THE HOT ROD

DEDICATION

To Duffy Livingstone, who made it all happen.

First published in 2003 by Motorbooks International, an imprint of
MBI Publishing Company, Galtier Plaza, Suite 200, 380 Jackson Street,
St. Paul, MN 55101-3885 USA

The information in this book is true and complete to the best of our
knowledge. All recommendations are made without any guarantee on the
part of the author or Publisher, who also disclaim any liability incurred in
connection with the use of this data or specific details.

We recognize that some words, model names and designations, for example,
mentioned herein are the property of the trademark holder. We use them for
identification purposes only. This is not an official publication.

Motorbooks International titles are also available at discounts in bulk quantity
for industrial or sales-promotional use. For details write to Special Sales
Manager at Motorbooks International Wholesalers & Distributors,
Galtier Plaza, Suite 200, 380 Jackson Street, St. Paul, MN 55101-3885 USA.

ISBN 0-7603-1598-1

On the front cover: Brock Yates collection
On the frontispiece: Steve Rossini
On the spine: Gordon Jolley
On the backcover: Angelo Lisuzzo

Editor: Darwin Holmstrom
Associate Editor: Peter Schletty
Editorial Assistant: Mariam Pourshoushtari
Designed by Tom Heffron

Printed in China

CONTENTS

ACKNOWLEDGMENTS

Special Thanks to these many friends for their contributions
to the ongoing Eliminator projects:

Duffy Livingstone
Barry Brown, Riter Restoration
Sam Tuner
Pete Chapouris, So-Cal Speed Shop
Pete Eastwood
Bob Jeffords, Riter Restoration
Jim Jeffords, Riter Restoration
Charles Henry
The staff of *Car and Driver*
Lou Patane and Mopar Performance

ACKNOWLEDGMENTS

Barry Gowen and Summit Race Shop
Bob Kennedy, Kennedy Automotive
Jim Browning and Corsa Performance
Todd Gartshore and Baer Brake Systems
Pat Ganahl
Ken Gross
Bert Skidmore
Tom Reece
Walt Bohren
Jim Sitz
Steve Oosterling
Jim Williams
Kirk F. White
Greg Sharp
Bill Edgar
Art Evans
Dick Vandervere
Tom Murphy
Jeff Gamble
David Pfost

Earl Pfost

Don Radbruch

Ernie Nagamatsu

Phil Davies

Howard Marter

Tom Medley

Thom Taylor

Buzz Shoemaker

The Tire Rack

Michelin Rubber Company

Alan Cape, Flying A Motorsports

TCI Engineering

Wescott Replicas

Bill Warner

And the understanding lady in the muddy dress.

INTRODUCTION

The American hot rod has become a cultural icon of the first magnitude. Dozens of motion pictures, surely headlined by George Lucas' *American Graffiti*, have sensationalized their role in the lifestyles of young men and woman. Once only described by decent folk as a ratty, ear-pounding highway menace, the hot rod has become a symbol of mechanical creativity and individual artistry with metal.

All manner of permutations of the machine now exist, including street rods, vintage rods, and the imported Japanese "rice burners" made famous in the Vin Diesel film *The Fast and the Furious*. The ultimate expression of home-built performance—300 mile-per-hour Top Fuel dragsters—can trace a direct lineage to the pioneer rodders of the 1930s.

Hot rodding has also spun off into the heady world of sports car racing, where such thoroughbred marques as

Ferrari, Porsche, Jaguar, Aston-Martin, and Bugatti have reigned for decades. Rodders had been quick to recognize the fun to be had, though, when road racing exploded in popularity following World War II. While hardly blessed with the exotic components found in the European machines, hot rodders in California had developed sufficient engine technology—first with the Ford flathead V-8 and then with a rash of short-stroke, overhead-valve V-8s developed by Detroit in the early 1950s—to enable them to compete on even term with the imports. In some cases, these "hot rods" stretched the terms to absurd lengths, as the magnificent Cunninghams did, resembling Europe's finest sports cars on the outside, yet carrying modified bits—engines, gearboxes, brakes—scavenged from American production cars.

Others with more limited budgets like Max Balchowsky, Ak Miller, Stirling Edwards, Ted Cannon, Chuck Manning, Willis Baldwin, Dick Morgenson, and Chuck Tatum, to name but a few, simply cobbled together bits and pieces of American production automobiles to create lightweight sports cars that were thinly disguised as hot rods.

One of the leaders in this group was a Pasadena muffler shop operator named Frank "Duffy" Livingstone. His Eliminator was little more than a lean-and-mean 1924 Ford Model-T roadster (known as a "T-bucket" in the trade) with a dirt-track sprint car suspension and American V-8 in its engine bay.

In 1956, I had seen the car race during my stint in the Navy and, through a strange set of circumstances, it reappeared in my life forty years later. With it came a lasting friendship with its creator and a wealth of experiences from the old car's re-exposure to both the world of hot rodding and sports car racing.

If nothing else, this story reaffirms the elemental truth that the world of automobile enthusiasm is occupied by wonderful and unique personalities involved with wonderful and unique automobiles. It is a world that I have been privileged to be part of for most of my life and which, in a small way, I hope to share with you.

—Brock Yates
Wyoming, New York

SECTION ONE
THE ROOTS OF HOT RODDING

THE HOT ROD

CHAPTER ONE
THE ELIMINATOR RETURNS

Perched on an open trailer in a Denny's parking lot outside Monterey, California, was a car that I have known about for over 40 years, had owned for nearly a year, and yet had not laid eyes on since the summer of 1956. Its presence was unique and unmistakable: a blocky, barebones body, stark white with red trim, on chunky, unfendered wheels, and, most riveting of all, with a bold number "184" painted in blaring red on its battered flanks. This was the Eliminator, about to return to the public after hiding out for decades in various southern California and Arizona race shops, garages, barns, and storage spaces. Once one of the most notorious southern California road racing hot rods, it had surfaced in a 1996 issue of *Hemmings Motor News*, (that incredible monthly treasure trove of unique and collectible automobiles). I had purchased it, sight unseen, from across the continent and then waited while it was restored by Pete Chapouris and his expert sidekick, Pete Eastwood, at Chapouris' elaborate PC3G (soon to be revived as the famed So-Cal Speed Shop) Pomona facility east of Los Angeles.

Now it was ready for an uncertain debut in the most prestigious vintage-car race in North America, the Monterey Historics at Laguna Seca. It had gained entry to the exclusive paddock thanks in part to the sharp memory of promoter Steve Earle, who as a kid had seen the Eliminator run at a variety of Cal·Club and Sports Car Club of America road races in the 1950s.

My wife Pamela and I had first flown west to Los Angeles, and then we drove north to Monterey for the race. Along the way, we passed the intersection of California state roads 41 and 446 where, south of the windswept hamlet of Cholame, perhaps the most famous car crash in history had occurred. There on September 30, 1955, James Dean had plowed his spanking new Porsche 550 Spyder into the flanks of college student Donald Turnupseed's Ford coupe.

To the north lies the lavish Monterey peninsula, where each August the elite of the exotic-car world gather for the Historic races as well as the world famous Pebble Beach Concours d'Elegance, a variety of high-dollar car auctions, and endless cocktail parties and corporate-sponsored receptions. It was into this heady world that Chapouris and Eastwood would bring the tatty but storied Eliminator.

We met them, as well as Chapouris' petite wife and business sidekick, Carol, over Denny's eggs and bacon and plotted our last-minute strategy. Chapouris' weekend would be full; the Eliminator would compete in the races while a few miles away, on the lush greenery of the famed Pebble Peach golf course, he was to display his masterpiece of restoration, a 1932 highboy hot rod belonging to noted California car collector and enthusiast Bruce Meyers. It would be the first time hot rods would be allowed to compete in the Concours, which had otherwise been the exclusive domain of such classics as Bugattis, Duesenbergs, Rolls-Royces, and other thoroughbreds.

Now, fresh out of Chapouris' Pomona shop would come a pair of interlopers, raging homebuilt invaders in the form of the Eliminator and Meyer's beautiful Deuce roadster, built in 1945 by the late, great California fabricator and race mechanic, Doane Spencer.

The first order of business was to nail down a race driver for the Eliminator. I was not a candidate. Following the death of our son, Sean, in September 1994, I had promised Pamela that my forays on the racetrack would end and had not driven competitively since. The original owner and builder of the car, Duffy Livingstone, was coming to Monterey and, while having wheeled the Eliminator with great skill before becoming a true immortal in the world of karting, at a sprightly 72 years he was a non-volunteer. Before the day was out, a driver would have to be enlisted or the trip to the Historics would be wasted.

I had originally recruited California sports car and drag racing ace Jim Busby, but he had later demurred, claiming concern for driving an ancient, leaf-sprung beast at speed. Considering his last serious racing had been at the wheel of

state-of-the-art Porsche 962 GTP coupes and 1970s vintage
Formula One cars, I couldn't really blame him. I had then
spoken with Lou Sellyei, a Reno, Nevada, ophthalmologist
and well-known Ferrari vintage racer, about the assign-
ment. Lou had ran in the 1975 Cannonball Sea-to-Shining-
Sea Memorial Trophy Dash with fellow doctor and vintage
racer Gary Arentz (carrying a box of pig eyes in an eye-bank
ruse that failed to help their cause when their Jaguar XJS
encountered mechanical troubles) and was known to be
game for strange challenges like driving the Eliminator. He
had originally consented, then backed out because his
Ferrari 250TR Testarossa would be competing in the same
race at the Historics.

Lou suggested letting Bert Skidmore, a young race driver
and excellent mechanic who ran Intrepid Motor Cars in
Reno, drive the Eliminator. His suggestion made sense. Part
of Bert's business involved maintaining both Lou and Tony
Wang's Ferraris, and he also drove Arentz's ex-Andretti
Lotus 79 Grand Prix car in vintage events. A phone conversation with Bert convinced me that he was a cool head and
highly qualified. However, his tone implied serious reservations about climbing behind the wheel of the old war-horse.

The paddock of the Laguna Seca road course during the
Historics weekend is a breathtaking car show unto itself. Part
of my duties for the weekend was to be on the announcing
team for the live television show being produced for the
Speedvision cable network (now Speed Channel). I would
have to spend hours interviewing owners and drivers of the
staggering collection of great racing cars assembled for the

races, ranging from early Alfa Romeo Grand Prix cars to the rare Maseratis and Ferraris that graced the starting grids in the 1950s. It would be against the latter groups of priceless and powerful cars that the Eliminator would compete, provided Skidmore would drive.

August weather patterns on the Monterey peninsula can be strangely predictable, and August of 1997 proved to be no exception. Early risers were greeted by a chill ocean breeze and dense fog on the higher elevations where the beautiful Laguna Seca racetrack had been carved out of land formerly belonging to the now vacated Fort Ord Army base. By the time Chapouris, Eastwood, and I had unloaded the car, set up a portable tent in our paddock space, and completed registration, the gray blanket above us had begun to clear and a bright sun made its all-day appearance.

Then the man who had unwittingly instigated the entire assault on the Monterey Historics arrived. Duffy Livingstone had driven down from his home in Grants Pass, Oregon, with his young wife, Dee Dee, to witness the resurrection of the car he had built and raced 40 years earlier. While I had spoken with him many times by phone during the car's restoration and sought advice on countless technical and historical points, this was my first meeting with a man whose name is a legend in the karting world.

Ruddy and clear-eyed, Duffy sported a loud, rouge-colored Hawaiian shirt similar to the one he had worn while racing the Eliminator in California sports car races four decades ago. "Duff" was warm and good humored and commented when he looked over the car, "Damn, the thing looks exactly like the last time I raced it against the sporty car guys. We used to call 'em 'tea baggers.' Made 'em mad as hell, but that only made it more fun."

Livingstone had ended his racing with the Eliminator to pioneer competition in the new world of karting and start his Azuza-based "Go-Kart" company—a name that would become synonymous with the exploding sport. His racing skills, honed with his old hot rod now hunkered down in the Laguna Seca paddock, had been transferred to major league karting competition, where he had become one of the fastest, hardest drivers among the karters. Recognizing his accomplishments, the International Karting Federation created the "Duffy Award," which remains one of the most coveted in the sport—a sport that now serves as ground zero for most of the top Grand Prix and Indy car drivers in the world.

Parked immediately across the paddock was a long, low, red trailer carrying the Intrepid Motosports logo. Two exquisite V12 Ferrari 250TR sports racing cars, one bright red, the other fly yellow, were parked outside. These were two of 33 such machines built between 1959 and 1961 in Maranello for international sports car competition and were two of the rarest vintage race cars on the planet.

The yellow TR was Tony Wang's, whose fortune, made in the computer business, afforded him sufficient financial comfort to risk exposing a rare, multi-million-dollar Ferrari to the vagaries of a racetrack. The other TR ("Testarossa," for the red-headed cam-covers favored by Enzo at the time) meant more to Livingstone. Its rakish, pontoon-fendered bodywork carried number 46, the same digits that had graced its flanks since the late 1950s. "I remember that car," mused Livingstone. "It belonged to Dick Morgensen, and he and I had a hell of a race at Santa Barbara in 1959. I'll never forget it."

It had indeed been a hell of a race. In the batch of material I had gathered up while researching the Eliminator, there was a photograph of Morgensen's Ferrari and Duffy's Eliminator battling in Santa Barbara. Here sat the two machines, essentially unchanged, 40 years later, ready to fight it out again. The reason: the driver of 46 was Lou Sellyei, who had turned down the Eliminator ride for the obvious reason that he was to drive his own car in the same race—a 10-lap sprint for sports racing cars built between 1955 and 1959.

The young man who ran Intrepid and maintained the Sellyei and Wang Ferraris sauntered across the paddock to look over the Eliminator. Bert Skidmore was lean, square-jawed, and built like a middleweight. Laconic and soft-spoken, he poked around the car, checking brake lines, oil fittings, throttle linkages, fuel line connections—all the essentials that made a race car safe—as Pete Eastwood, a classic California hot rod genius, stood by, confident his craftsmanship would pass inspection.

It did. Skidmore nodded approval and agreed to drive the Eliminator. We were ready to race once the formal inspection by the HMSA (Historic Motor Sports Association) that ran the Historics was conducted. Heading for inspection, Eastwood climbed into the Eliminator and fired it up, its Chevy V-8 that had been carefully assembled at the Ohio-based Summit Racing Equipment shop blatting impudently. A small crowd gathered as he jammed the car into gear and rumbled off.

It was instantly apparent that the old beast was to be the source of controversy and fascination at Monterey. Some gaped in amazement at the battered, T-bucket bodywork. Others turned their heads away, as if viewing a bad accident, while many smiled openly at the outrageous interloper. Duffy, who had brought along his camcorder and was burning tape at a furious rate, stood away from the crowd and was not thought to be part of the barbarian band who had arrived with the car. This permitted him to overhear a bejeweled little woman in starched Bermuda shorts and a straw hat sneer, "I don't understand why they let that thing run with our cars."

The Eliminator passed inspection, but only after Eastwood was asked to install an extra crankcase overflow container. In keeping with the theme of the car, he chose not a modern, spun-aluminum product, but rather an empty Marvel Mystery Oil quart can.

It somehow perfectly fit the theme of the Eliminator: a 1925 Ford T-Bucket-bodied hot rod lavished with such 1930s race car technology as Ford drum brakes, hydraulic, lever-controlled Houdaille shock absorbers, late 1920s Dodge steering, transverse leaf-spring suspension fore and aft, and a rail frame from a wrecked 1929 Ford sedan. Facing it would be race cars easily thirty years more advanced in technology: Peter Hardman's exquisite 1959 Aston-Martin DBR1; Rob Walton's Tipo 61 Birdcage

Maserati; John Harden, Vic Edelbrock, and David Reynolds' Lister Corvettes; Murray Smith's Chaparral I; two D-type Jaguars of Archie Urciuolo and Edurado Baptista; and, no less, five 250TR Ferraris, including Sellyei's and Wang's. Most carried disc brakes; advanced, lightweight tubular or monocoque chassis; and wind-cheating, featherweight aluminum or fiberglass bodywork. Only two slightly ancient hot rods in the field bore resemblance to the Eliminator: Dr. Ernie Nagamatsu's famous, ex-Max Balchowsky Ol' Yeller II and Bill Jankowski's Monsterati, a California-based hot rod racer with primitive underpinnings like the Eliminator.

Group 4B, as our race field was named, had its first practice session on Friday morning prior to the 10-lap, 25 miler set for the following afternoon. The Laguna Seca grandstand would be jammed with fans who would then, according to tradition, drift off on Sunday to the nearby Pebble Beach Concours.

Skidmore warily climbed into the cramped cockpit of the Eliminator, lit up the big V-8, and chugged off to the pits to line up for practice. The shift from his customary drive in the ex-Andretti Lotus 79 GP car to the ancient Eliminator was like stepping from an F16 Fighter to a World War I Spad biplane.

The green flag dropped and he puttered around the swooping, beautifully manicured circuit for six easy laps and came in. Other than commenting about the insanely vague steering, he seemed content and vowed to up the pace in the second practice session later that day.

We were unaware that he had just ran in the qualifying session for the race. When the times were posted, we were listed as the 18th starter in a 19-car field. Only David Reynolds, who had encountered mechanical troubles with his Lister-Jaguar, was slower. Peter Hardman and Rob Walton, gridded one and two, seemed miles ahead on time in their Aston and Maserati masterpieces.

Considering this was the first time the Eliminator had rolled a wheel in anger in over forty years and that Skidmore thought the old nail had more in it with some extra practice, not all seemed lost.

A second session brought some satisfaction as he began to develop a comfort level with the car and lap times began to plunge. The vintage Dunlop radials, required for all cars in the race, were beginning to scrub in and, after some jiggling with tire pressures and a few adjustments on the three 1930s-vintage Stromberg 97 carburetors, the Eliminator began to show some muscle. Skidmore commented quietly that he was amazed at how well the old beast handled. We began to think perhaps humiliation levels during the race might not be as high as we feared.

Among the curious who swarmed around the car was Max Balchowsky, himself the most famous of the California hot rodder-cum-road racers, whose famed Buick-powered Ol' Yellers (named after the 1957 motion picture) competed against and often beat the best Ferraris and Maseratis of the late 1950s. Max, now in his late 70s but still wearing his trademark zip-up coveralls, had known Duffy since the old days. Both could recall a time when they made chassis designs by drawing outlines in chalk on their shop floors and employed raw improvisation to create fast automobiles.

The field lined up for Saturday's 10-lapper two-by-two for the rolling start. Skidmore, at the back, scrambled off the final, tight left-hander onto the main straight as Hardman and Walton took the green flag. Suddenly, the Eliminator came to life. The old machine thundered past the start-finish line and, before Skidmore reached the tricky double-down-hill left leading into the infield, he had nailed his patron, Sellyei, in his Ferrari and was now on the tail of Nagamatsu in Ol' Yeller. By the second lap, he had moved up three spots, elbowing past another pair of Ferraris and a Maserati 200Si.

The Eliminator was on the prowl.

By the fourth lap, Bert had burst into 12th place, and the track announcers began to follow the car. "Skidmore just got another five million dollars worth of Italian thoroughbreds," they screeched over the PA. The crowd began to respond, waving and cheering as the old crock moved through the field. Hardman was well out in front, driving masterfully with the Aston and well on his way to victory. But it was the Eliminator that captured the attention of the throng, who hooted and yelled it forward as Skidmore steadily picked off cars.

Duffy and I stood on the edge of the track, beaming as the Eliminator showed its heels to radically more advanced and modern machinery. "Damn, that old thing runs just as good as it did 40 years ago," Livingstone mused over the din.

Ten laps did not offer much opportunity for serious racing, but by the time the checkered flag fell, Skidmore had advanced 10 positions to eighth place. Within a few more laps, it would have caught at least three more cars. In all, an amazing and totally exhilarating performance for the old car and its young driver.

As he rolled back into the paddock, the car was enveloped by enthusiasts who wanted a close-up look at the unlikely beast. Not among them was the bejeweled wife who had sneered so openly. Her husband was one of the four Ferrari TR drivers who had been overwhelmed by the interloper.

One of the Ferrari drivers sauntered over to Skidmore, who was basking in praises. "You're fired," announced Lou Sellyei with a broad grin on his face. Sellyei, whose droll sense of humor was well known in West Coast vintage racing circles, was at best a casual racer, understandably reluctant to flog his multi-million-dollar Ferraris for the sake of a silver trophy or a few post-race back-slaps. While his suspension of Skidmore's services was regarded as a big joke, the underlying message was clear: the Eliminator had burst onto the rarified world of exotic vintage-car racing with a large bang.

Among the onlookers was Bob Cumberford, a highly respected journalist and automotive designer whose credentials could be traced to the Zora-Arkus Duntov team that had developed the early Corvettes for General Motors. Cumberford, along with such prodigies as Cobra designer Peter Brock and the late Larry Shinoda, had all subsequently risen to the top in the world of high-performance automobiles. Now a regular columnist for *Automobile Magazine*, Cumberford had spotted the Eliminator's superb handling during the race where it had cornered, flat and true, on Laguna's challenging layout.

Cumberford kneeled down and examined the car's rear suspension. With four links and a Panhard bar, it was much more complex and sophisticated than it seemed, shrouded as it was under the ancient Model-T bodywork. "Very interesting," he said to Duffy. "It's great the way you mounted the transverse leaf-spring so far behind the rear axle. It does great things to improve the roll center."

"Yeah it works great," said Duffy casually. "I wish I'd designed it that way. Actually, we only built it so the rear spring would clear the Halibrand quickchange."

So much for high-technology on the Eliminator.

Then Chapouris rushed into the paddock, driving his beautiful lime green 1929 Ford roadster and smiling widely. The Bruce Meyer entry, his Doane Spencer highboy, had won the Dean Batchelor Memorial Trophy at Pebble Beach among an extraordinary field of entries that, for the first time at the renowned Concours d'Elegance, celebrated the uniquely American hot rod-building art.

Chapouris, Bert, Duffy and Dee Dee, Pete Eastwood, and Pamela and I basked in the late afternoon sunshine, accepting the congratulations for the Eliminator's great run and Pete and Bruce's triumph at Pebble Beach.

The fun was hardly over. Monterey Historics impresario Steve Earle conducted his traditional awards ceremony that, unlike most races, did not necessarily honor the winners, but rather cars and drivers who best exemplified the spirit of the vintage motor racing. When it came time to recognize the best performance in Race 4B, he called out number 184. I stepped out of the crowd to accept a beautiful Chopard chronograph inscribed with the date—August 15, 1997—on behalf of the entire crew. Truly, it was one of the most memorable moments in my long and crazy life around motor racing, and I wear the Chopard with pride to this day.

When Monday came, Skidmore and his Intrepid crew loaded up the Wang and Sellyei Ferraris and headed back to Reno. Chapouris and Eastwood drove back to Los Angeles while Duffy and Dee Dee drove north to the Oregon coast.

I had one more mission before leaving Monterey. The Eliminator had to be shipped back to my home in upstate New York. Passport Transportation, one of the top exotic car shippers in the nation, had been enlisted to haul it in one of its giant green-and-yellow semis specially rigged for such rare and fragile freight.

The Laguna Seca pits were nearly empty come Monday morning, save for a few trailers, some clean-up crews, and a row of Passport, Reliable, and InterCity rigs ready for east-bound runs. I wedged myself behind the wheel of the Eliminator, although my height and shoe size made serious driving nearly impossible, and chugged it across the paddock to a giant Passport transporter. Its driver, a paunchy man with a million hard road miles under his belt, looked over the car. He carried a clipboard with a Passport form that, like all such company's, required him to record all dings, dents, scratches, and body damage prior to loading in order to avoid liability.

One problem: the Eliminator's ancient bodywork was a spider-web of faded paint and battered metal. The driver began to write.

The Eliminator's owner, old and new. Duffy Livingstone and Yates in the Monterey pits. *Pat Ganahl*

Skidmore at speed.

The Eliminator handles the Laguna's dreaded corkscrew flat and true.
Peter Brock

Bert Skidmore and Duff Livingstone discuss tactics.

Skidmore warms the car prior to his first tentative practice.

The start. Skidmore would pass all the cars in front of him within five laps!

Yates describes the car for the Speedvision television network.

The Eliminator leads the Sellyei Ferrari 250 TR through the corkscrew.

The Cal Club Goleta trials in 1949. Roger Barlow's Talbot T150 leads the earliest hot rod road racer, Phil Payne's Baldwin Special, followed by Johnny Von Neumann in a second Talbot. *Jack Campbell: Edgar Motorsport Archive*

sports car exhaust service ★
fibre-glass packed mufflers ★

Duff & Roy's
MUFFLER SHOP
specializing in QUIET, efficient header systems

803 E. COLORADO
PASADENA, CALIF.
SY. 2-9378

"world's most famous"

A business card and Christmas card from Duff and Roy's and
GP Muffler shops.

𝔜uletide 𝔊reetings

1954

G P MUFFLER & MFG.

MONROVIA, CALIFORNIA

Xmas 1954

No trailer here. Duff's Model-A towed the Eliminator to the races.

Duffy and his Caddy-powered hot rod at Muroc dry lakes in 1948. His best run was just over 110 miles per hour. The drives to and from the Lakes were the most fun.
Livingstone collection

The bare-boned Eliminator nearly completed in 1954.

The curious examine the newly arrived Eliminator at Palm Springs in 1954.

Paul Parker angles the Eliminator into a Santa Barbara corner as another special spins.
The photo was taken by Ferrari enthusiast and team owner John Edgar on September 5, 1954.
Edgar Motorsport Archive

"Put your pen away," I said. "Don't bother. This old rascal is original, warts and all. The dents are part of its charm."

"Man, that's a relief," said the driver as he tucked his clipboard under his arm. "I'd have been here for a week marking down the scratches on this thing. Most of the guys I haul cars for are so anal they get nuts if there's a fingerprint on the paint."

"Load her up. I'll see you back east," I said.

And so ended the resurrection of the Eliminator. It was hardly the end, though, but rather only a chapter in the nearly century-long history of an automotive phenomenon known as the American hot rod.

CHAPTER TWO
DUSTY BEGINNINGS

The source of the slang "hot rod" remains lost in time. Some historians claim it was a pejorative dreamed up by a long-forgotten headline writer at the Hearst-owned Los Angeles *Herald* or *Examiner* newspapers sometime in the mid-1940s. The two dailies were notorious for slandering all forms of motorsport, presenting them as deadly diversions undertaken only by the suicidal and the speed-perverted. Others believe it was conjured up by someone who simply abbreviated "hot roadster" into a usable contraction.

Some are convinced it was first used immediately prior to World War II, while many historians maintain there is no written evidence that it was in common usage until young veterans returned home in 1945. What is recorded is the enthusiasm for high-performance roadsters, coupes, and sedans that first arose in the late 1910s across the nation and, in particular, in the car-crazy Los Angeles basin. Huge western migrations, mainly from the Midwest and South, had transformed Los Angeles from a sunny but semi-arid desert settlement into a booming metropolis. For the most part, these immigrants made the trek to Los Angeles aboard automobiles, vehicles perfectly suited for movement around the vast avenues and wide streets gridded at the base of the San Gabriel and Santa Monica mountains surrounding the new paradise. The motion picture industry, lured by the endless summer, quickly created vast wealth out of the wilderness and a concurrent enthusiasm for the cranky, expensive but chic new automobiles.

Motorsports in the United States had until 1909 been limited to European-style road racing for prizes like the Vanderbilt and Elgin Cups, as well as competitions on the myriad of mile and half-mile horse ovals that dotted every town, city, and village in the nation. Then came the revolutionary Indianapolis Motor Speedway in 1909, an immense 2.5-mile rectangle that inspired a mass of new track developers, including European-educated Fred Moscovics who would later become the President of the Stutz Motor Company. His entry into racetrack construction came in concert with ex-British bicycle racing champion Jack Prince's construction of small, high-banked, wooden "velodromes" across the nation for pedal-powered competition.

Moscovics, who had managed the Mercedes-Benz team during an American foray to run the Vanderbilt Cup, had an audacious idea perfectly suited to the Hollywood theatrics that blossomed around him: simply enlarge Prince's plans for wooden bicycle tracks into a monster bowl for automobiles. His pie-plated circle would be one-mile long, 45-feet wide, and banked 20 degrees. This would be the world's first 100-mile-per-hour track, claimed Moscovics, and he made a friendly wager with car manufacturer Howard Marmon that automobiles would routinely lap his speedway beyond the century mark. At this time, automobiles still dawdled around the newly-built, lumpy-brick Indianapolis Motor Speedway at little more than 80 miles per hour.

The Moscovics-Prince Motordrome was built at Playa del Rey, a small resort area near Venice, west of the booming city of Los Angeles, and reachable by the ever-expanding Pacific Electric light-rail line spidering across the basin. The Motordrome would be built out of millions of board feet of 2-by-4 Douglas Fir boards laid end-to-end on a spindly framework. The idea was revolutionary and seized the imaginations of racetrack builders from coast to coast. In all, 24 board tracks would be built in the 1920s. Despite the rush to build, all would be gone—rotted away, burned up, or torn down—by the end of the decade.

The Motordrome opened in the spring of 1910 with superstar Barney Oldfield attempting to lap the saucer (dubbed the "pie pan" by the local press) at 100 miles per hour. He failed by a few hundredths of a second and the barrier would never be crossed during the three years the track operated. In 1913, it caught fire and burned to the ground, prompting nationally-syndicated columnist Ring Lardner—who, like most major sporting figures of the day, hated the dangerous, often lethal new sport of auto racing—to muse, "Playa del Rey burned down last night, with a great saving of lives."

World War I would have to play out its macabre drama in the European trenches before another attempt to revive board tracks in southern California would be undertaken. In 1920, a group of area investors created the most elegant wooden speedway of them all. It would border tree-lined Wilshire Boulevard in Beverly Hills and sit on the corner of Beverly Drive. Beverly Drive was hardly the canyon of elegant office buildings and hotels it is today, rather a vast flatland west of the burgeoning suburb. The new track would not be a duplication of the saucer that had been stilted up in Playa del Rey, but rather a true, high-speed rectangle 1.25 miles in length and highlighted by a massive, roofed grandstand lining its front straightaway. Built with the grandeur and outré elegance that symbolized the movie colony of the day, the new Los Angeles Motor Speedway consumed 193 acres and was erected in just five weeks by a legion of workers. The sweeping corners, banked at 35 degrees, employed a spiral easement principle, first developed for railroads, that allowed a smooth transition from the corners to the long straightaway.

Unlike the Moscovics-Prince Motordrome, which was too far away from the Los Angeles population center (freeways had not even been imagined in those days) and never enjoyed large crowds, the new Speedway was a major success from the opening green flag. The infield was so vast that aviation meets were held in connection with the races. Monoplanes and multi-engine monsters chugged into the air from a runaway that paralleled the back straight.

Despite its popularity, the track would die not from a lack of support. Rather it was exploding real estate values, caused in part by the construction of what historian Howard Osmer labeled "Pickfair," the mansion of film idols Douglas Fairbanks and Mary Pickford in the Santa Monica hills overlooking the Speedway, that caused its demise. The Beverly Hills population in 1920 was 674 souls. A decade later, it was 17,429, the result of the fantastic new movie industry and the men and woman who had become instant millionaires due to its success. By 1924, the land over which the Los Angeles Motor Speedway sprawled had become so valuable that the owners had no choice but to accede to real estate developers and sell. Like all the racetracks that were to fall victim to the crazed escalation of land values in the Los Angeles basin, the great track was sawed to bits, its lumber converted to thousands of bungalows and cottages that would dot its lost acreage.

Today there are few people still living who have actually seen the Speedway. It must have been a sight: the stupendous, high-banked track, dark and shimmering brown, streaked with oil and skid marks left by squadrons of thundering, smoking, circus-painted automobiles, their spinning wire wheels blinking in the bright California sunlight, circulating like low-flying, tropical birds; the sweet aroma of the fresh-cut timbers mixing with castor oil and alcohol fumes wafted into the giant, roofed grandstands packed with tailored men and well-coifed ladies, the distant, snow-capped peaks of the proud mountains in the background. Nowhere in history of the sport has such a scene of opulent, high-powered competition been duplicated.

Only one serious crash occurred during the four-year tenure of the Los Angeles Motor Speedway, and one of its victims would have a major influence, if obliquely, in the development of the California car craze. Gaston Chevrolet was one of three Swiss-born, French-raised brothers who had come to the United States prior to 1900 to establish themselves in the fledging automobile industry, both in terms of motorsport and passenger car construction. Their story is long, involved, and spotted with triumph and failure.

On Thanksgiving Day in 1920, the best race drivers in the business arrived at Beverly Hills for a 250-mile contest, where Gaston Chevrolet's victory in the Indianapolis 500 earlier that May would be celebrated. He would be at the wheel of his own Monroe-Frontenac, a bulbous nosed, two-man machine developed in in concert with his brothers, Arthur and Louis. On the 160th lap, Gaston was sailing through the third turn of the big oval at well over 120 miles-per-hour when his Monroe touched wheels with Eddie O'Donnell's Duesenberg. The Duesy spun wickedly and was sent skating toward the outer wall where it pitched O'Donnell's riding mechanic, Lyall Jolls, over the side, plunging him 50 feet to his death. Chevrolet's car tumbled madly down the track. While his mechanic, Johnnie Bresnahan, was thrown clear and escaped with minor injuries, the great star was killed instantly. O'Donnell, gravely injured, survived a few hours before becoming the third victim of the tragedy.

Though the best known of the Chevrolet brothers was gone, their legacy would live on—most famously for the car named after them (the rights for which they had sold in 1914 to William Crapo Durant and his fledging General Motors Corporation for a piddling $1,500)—but also for their Ford Frontenac engines that would be a basic ingredient for a nascent high-performance industry.

By 1920, Henry Ford—the biggest name in America's rapidly growing auto industry—had sold well over 10 million Model T's. The "Tin Lizzie" had literally caused a sea change in the American way of life and formed a foundation for massive expansion of automobile racing and automotive enthusiasm in general.

In 1918, Robert Roof, a visionary machinist in Anderson, Indiana, developed and marketed through local Laurel Motors both eight- and 16-valve conversion cylinder heads for the four-cylinder Ford T-block. The Roof-Ford became an instant player on the dirt tracks of the Midwest and soon made its way to California, where performance nuts attached them to their Model-T passenger cars. Roof conversions also went south, helping bootleggers elude government revenuers in the Great Smokey hills and hollows above the Piemont Plateau.

The first eight-valve Roof cylinder head bumped the Ford four-banger from a rated 17 horsepower to nearly 33. The later 16-valve version was substantially stronger and began to appear in major races as a competitor to the exotic Duesenbergs, Millers, Ballots, Fiats, and Peugeots that dominated big-time motorsports.

Selling for $998.25, the Roof conversion was a Wal-Mart-priced entrée into racing. By the end of the 1920s, when competitors entered the market, Laurel Motors had produced more than 10,000. Major competition would come from the two remaining Chevrolet brothers, who began to produce both eight- and 16-valve conversions for the Model-T block under the Frontenac name. Their "Fronty Fords," as they became known throughout the racing fraternity, were amazing devices.

In 1923, L.L. "Slim" Corum, driving for a local Indianapolis Ford dealer called Barber-Warnock, piloted his Frontenac-Ford to fifth place in the "500," averaging 82.5 miles per hour. In the process, he finished ahead of no less than eight Bugattis, three Mercedes, seven Millers, three Packards, and a Duesenberg, all radically more exotic and expensive than his tarted-up T. That same year, a French team trundled home 14th with a Frontenac-Ford powered Montier in the first Le Mans 24 Hours endurance race.

In many ways, the Fronty-Ford, the Roofs, and similar Indiana-based conversions from Morton and Brett, Craig-Hunt, the famous Rajo (a contraction of its designer and maker, Joe Jagersburger and his hometown of Racine, Wisconsin, where the cylinder heads were manufactured), and others, were the reason why grassroots motorsport thrived in the 1920s and, more importantly, survived into the 1930s.

These increasingly potent Ford conversions were employed primarily in single-seat cars racing on dirt tracks around the nation. But in southern California, another application was favored, unique to the climate and terrain of that energetic region. In the high desert to the north and east of Los Angeles, lie a series of dry lakes, table-flat expanses of

arid earth that were ideal for high-speed driving with modified stock cars and racing machines of all kinds.

Too small for the outright land speed record attempts that
were still being run on the Daytona-Ormond Beach in North
Florida or on the Pendine Sands in Wales, dry lakes like
Muroc, Mojave, Rosamond, El Mirage, Harper, and Russetta
were well suited for modified roadsters and sedans capable of
100 miles per hour—a velocity considered hypersonic for a
passenger car in the 1920s.

This dry lakes hobby would remain only marginally interesting to Los Angeles racing fans. Another board track—the
ultimate bowl—would rise from the devastating loss of the
Los Angeles Motor Speedway in 1924. Within the frenzied
month of November of that year, the indefagitable Jack Prince
and his associates threw up a super-speedway in Culver City
on the southern edge of the sprawling MGM movie lot. Like
Los Angeles Motor Speedway, it would also be 1.25 miles in
length but with radical 45-degree banked corners. The
straightaways would be longer and the turns slightly tighter,
permitting what was hoped to be the first 150 mile-per-hour
laps on a closed course. However, this was not to be, although
on March 6, 1927, Frank Lockhart, one of the true geniuses of
American motorsport, came close driving his 91-cubic-inch,
supercharged and intercooled Miller straight-8 around Culver
City at the stunning average of 144.200 miles per hour—a
speed that would not be equaled until 30 years later!

Again, the Kudzu-like encroachment of Los Angeles real
estate doomed the Culver City track, and it fell to the saws
and bulldozers of construction crews at the end of 1927.

Sadly, Lockhart would never reach his much deserved peak in the pantheon of motorsports. Later in 1927, he took the same supercharged Miller 91 single-seater Indy car to Muroc Dry Lake in the Mojave Desert and ran 172 miles per hour—only 32 miles per hour short of the absolute land speed record held by a car powered by a British aircraft engine *thirty times* larger in displacement. Encouraged by the attempt, Lockhart, whose brilliance was indicated by record-shattering test scores he received when applying for the famed California Institute of Technology, built the tiny, bullet-shaped V-16 Stutz Black Hawk to gain the outright record. But on April 25, 1928, while running a record-setting 220 miles per hour on the Daytona Beach sands, a tire blew and the brilliant driver died in the ensuing tumble. Still, Frank Lockhart will be remembered as one of the first of many dazzlingly creative, self-taught driver-engineers to rise out of southern California and shake the automotive world to its core.

It had been standard practice in the Detroit-based industry to paint their boxy sedans and coupes in drab, basic colors with only rudimentary trim. Henry Ford's famous crack about his Model-T—"You can have any color, as long as it's black"—served as the mantra for the entire business.

In California, the booming motion picture industry had created a demand for more vivid shapes and colors among a clientele vastly more audacious and flamboyant than the average consumer. To meet this demand, Los Angeles Cadillac dealer Don Lee had hired young Harley J. Earl, the son of a coach-builder, to customize Cadillacs and other exotic luxury cars for screen stars and film moguls.

Earl, a lanky, larger-than-life character, began fitting low, rakish bodies to otherwise subdued sedans and roadsters and lavishing them with lurid, two-and-three-tone paint treatments.

On a trip to Los Angeles in 1927, Lawrence Fisher, one of the brothers whose company had built all the bodies for General Motors, visited the Lee dealership and was bowled over by Earl's outré styling themes. He immediately saw tremendous potential in the young man and lured him to Detroit where Earl created the General Motors "Art and Color Section" in 1928.

Harley J. Earl and his small staff, which was soon to include Bill Mitchell and other brilliant designers, would blossom into the massive design staff for GM and energize automobile styling around the world. Earl would later create the incredible finned Cadillacs of the postwar era, the first Corvettes, and dozens of other breakthrough designs that, according to most historians, would make General Motors dominant in the worldwide industry for nearly half a century. The mother lode of this power can be traced to Earl and the sun-drenched expanses of southern California.

While the board tracks and the former horse tracks at Ascot Park on Avalon Boulevard were the centers of sanctioned auto racing, hundreds of enthusiasts began to join Lockhart and others on the dry lakes for informal races. They probably began in the early 1920s, although historians have been unable to pin down exactly when the first car raised dust on a California dry lake. What is known is that by the middle of the twenties, racing had become quasi-formal, with small clubs organizing the competition. The simple, straight-line, head-to-head races had resembled the "drags" that would become popular following World War II (although the phase "drag racing" would be unknown until the late 1930s or early 1940s).

The lake races would sometimes involve as many as six cars, all blazing across the hard dirt until one would clearly establish itself as the fastest. Crude timing equipment had been developed that could measure top speed on individual cars, and serious, purpose-built dry lakes speedsters had begun to appear.

As the Depression descended on the nation in 1930 and the great board tracks faded to fond memories, more and more California enthusiasts began to devote what small budgets they had to modifying their passenger cars for street and dry lakes competition.

In 1926, hard-headed, old Henry Ford finally relented and stopped building his beloved Model T, which by that time numbered 15 million units. After an agonizing near 18-month production hiatus ceased, the eccentric genius introduced his Model A, a cleaner, more advanced machine carrying a 200-cubic-inch flathead four-cylinder producing 40 horsepower. In 1932, the Model B was introduced, having 10 more horsepower and pressurized oil lubrication and fuel supply. The Model B became an instant favorite for engine builders in California and in the Midwest and made a potent competitor both on American dirt tracks and on the dry lakes.

Special flathead Model-B cylinder heads were manufactured by such luminaries as the Winfield brothers, Ed and

W.C. "Bud," whose names are most closely associated with custom camshafts, carburetors, and the legendary Novi V-8. A fresh batch of double-and-single overhead cylinder heads would be offered by scores of designers, including the great Harry Miller (due to a series of business miscues, his design ended up being offered first by Miller-Schofield, and then by Crane Plumbing heir, Crane Garth, under the famed Cragar label). Los Angeles-based George Riley built excellent OHV Model B versions as did D. O. Hal, McDowell, Dryer, Rajo, and Gemsa, among others.

The four-cylinder Model B conversions flexed their muscles both on the dry lakes and on the infamous Legion Ascot five-eighths-mile dirt track, where overhead and camshaft Cragar and Riley conversions were able to battle against the full-race Millers and Offenhausers.

A vast inventory of speed equipment became available for the Model B's, such as intake and exhaust manifolds, camshafts, carburetors, and ignition systems. This variety of high-performance parts prompted the opening of several specialty shops. The most famous of these were Lee Chapel's store on the San Fernando Road north of the city and George Wight's Bell Auto Parts, which had grown out of a junkyard specializing in Model-T bits and pieces, located on Gage Avenue in Bell, California. Chapel would remain a fixture in the sport, even after he moved his shop north to Oakland. But it was a historical footnote compared to Wight's business that had rose to worldwide fame in the hands of Roy Richter, a brilliant fabricator, race car builder, and businessman. Under Richter's leadership, the little shop—now closed—radiated outward in two directions. The Cragar name became a famous brand for custom wheels and other accessories, while the Bell brand thrives to this day on helmets and other racing safety equipment .

By the early 1930s, the Los Angeles basin was a hot-bed of high performance. Not only was Harry Miller building great racing cars, but his shop foreman, Fred Offenhauser, was on the verge of taking over his star-crossed boss' business. Offenhauser began building engines for Indianapolis competition as well as the new craze in midget racing. Offenhauser's success prompted oil baron Earl Gilmore to construct an 18,000 seat, horseshoe-shaped stadium for both midget racing and football games on the corner of Beverly Boulevard and Fairfax Avenue west of downtown Los Angeles in 1934. "Gilmore" was an instant hit, with packed crowds cheering the nighttime midget races as well as LA's first pro-football team, the Bulldogs.

The midget racing crowd consisted of a wild mixture of hot rodders, professional race drivers, engine builders, fabricators, and promoters, all of whom prospered during the midget craze that lasted until the late 1940s. Again, real estate pressures doomed Gilmore, and it was razed in 1951, ultimately to be replaced by the CBS television studios and the Los Angeles Farmers Market.

At the time Gilmore was built, the greatest single influence in hot rodding had been on the market for two years. Henry Ford's Model B four-cylinder was being challenged by General Motors' Chevrolet six, when the eccentric old billionaire went for broke with his 1932 V-8, the world's first affordable V-8 engine and one of the greatest production powerplants in history.

Ford's 3.6-liter flathead developed a modest 65 horsepower, but was instantly embraced by the dry-lakes crowd as the engine of the future. A flood of speed equipment poured onto the market: aluminum cylinder heads from Eddie Meyer; Spalding, Kong, and Mallory high-intensity ignitions; Edelbrock and Weiand intake manifolds; and Winfield cams. Scores of other speed equipment producers, all operating out of small machine shops, backyard garages, gas-station service bays, and basement workshops sprang up to serve the ever-increasing legions of racers who headed into the high desert each weekend for a lash-up of flat-out lakes running.

Despite all this speed-related activity, the Depression had wreaked havoc on the car industry and automobile racing in particular. The board-track phenomenon was over. Miller was heading toward oblivion and the rival Duesenberg works were on the rocks as well.

In a desperate attempt to stay in business, the American Automobile Association and the Indianapolis Motor Speedway adopted the so-called "junk formula" that allowed large displacement passenger-car engines to compete in championship competition, which had devolved into a handful of one-mile dirt-track races and the prestigious "500."

Yet enthusiasm for high-performance automobiles refused to be crushed under the mountain of debt and pessimism gripping the nation. Ford's new flathead V-8, quickly dubbed the "bent eight" by the southern California racing crowd, energized the lakes competition, and, by 1932, hundreds of cars made the treks to Muroc and Rosamond each weekend.

It was dangerous business. Young men with little or no formal engineering training were modifying, or "souping up," family passenger coupes and sedans to run perhaps twice as fast as what was intended on their flimsy wheels and flabby suspensions. As the speeds escalated beyond 100 miles per hour, accidents became common. Cars flipped and rolled across the burnt-umber landscape. Injuries, some fatal, were common. With no medical or police services within a day's drive, there were instances when a young victim's body would be left on the steps of the Rosamond, California, post office.

Clubs formed to race on the lakes and to contest each other for top-speed honors. Into this scene entered a future giant of the sport. He was a native Oklahoman named Wally Parks who, like most of his compatriots, had come west with his family as a teenager. Parks made several trips to Muroc to observe the action and then came back in 1933 with a slightly modified Chevrolet Convertible that was clocked a credible 82 miles per hour. Hooked on the sport, he joined the Road Runners, one of the largest and most active of the Los Angeles car clubs.

As the performance business expanded and more clubs formed to race on the dry lakes, disputes developed over what rules, if any, were to regulate the competition. By 1937, the animosity reached a level where cooler heads, including Parks', organized a peace parlay among seven clubs that included the

Desert Goats, Night Fliers, 90 MPH club, the Ramblers, Glendale Sidewinders, Hollywood Throttlers, and the Road Runners. From this truce arose the Southern California Timing Association, which slowly absorbed such smaller organizations like the Muroc Racing Association and the Western Timing Association. Before the war scattered their members, a total of 38 high-performance clubs had joined the SCTA.

In 1938, Parks began to edit the club's *SCTA Racing News*, a small newsletter that spread the word throughout the Los Angeles basin. It is believed by some historians that Parks was first to use the term "drag race" in print in the March 1, 1939, issue of the *News*.

While California's balmy weather and the unique geography of the high-desert dry lakes is generally credited with the rise of what would soon be called the "hot rod" movement, the contribution of the southern California aircraft industry is sometimes ignored. In the vast region bordered by the Santa Monica Mountains and the Pacific Ocean was the powerful and ever-expanding commercial- and military-aircraft construction business. Entrepreneurs including Donald Douglas, Jack Northrup, Glenn Martin, Gerard Vultee, and others settled in Los Angeles and its environs to create monster firms like Douglas, Lockheed, Martin, Consolidated-Vultee, and Northrup. Within those empires thousands of young men were trained in every phase of high-tech manufacturing: welding, tool- and die-making, machining, metalworking. They formed a core of skilled enthusiasts who, on their off-hours, built automobiles and accessories for the street and the dry lakes.

Some technology spilled over directly from the aircraft business to the racers. A few attempts at streamlined cars appeared at Muroc and elsewhere, but were too heavy to break any records. Meanwhile, men like Stuart Hillborn, Vic Edelbrock, the aforementioned Ed Winfield, Phil Remington, and others were fabricating open-wheel machines that were turning speeds approaching 150 miles per hour—a prodigious velocity considering the level of stock automobiles and parts available to workaday guys in the late 1930s.

At the same time, street racing was beginning to reach levels that caused concern among the elite establishment. The late Dean Batchelor recounts an incident in his excellent history, *The American Hot Rod*, wherein young Bob Estes, driving his Frontenac-modified 1925 Model-T, blew away superstar Clark Gable's V-12 Packard in a series of stoplight races down Santa Monica Boulevard. Estes, who grew up to become a prominent Los Angeles car dealer and a regular entrant at the Indianapolis 500, was but one of hundreds of enthusiasts wheeling cars around the city with performance that positively stunned owners of expensive, seemingly unbeatable machinery like Gable's Packard.

As the clouds of war descended on the nation in late 1940 and the Japanese rained death on Pearl Harbor in December 1941, the California aircraft industry would play a major role in the ultimate victory over Japan and Germany. Scores of hardcore automobile enthusiasts would either work in that massive industry or serve in the armed forces, where their technical skills and their intuitive handiwork with machinery would be exploited by the military.

Ironically, the two worlds of the nascent hot rodders and the aircraft industry would clash on the dried mud flats of Muroc in 1938. The largest and smoothest of the vast high desert expanses, Muroc was also favored by the Army Air Corps as a testing site. Using government muscle, the fliers ejected the racers from the lakebed, though they relented slightly and let them run there on a limited basis until early 1942 when it was closed completely. The entire area is now called Rogers Dry Lake and lies within the perimeters of the legendary, ultra-secret Edwards Air Force test center.

As the dust settled on Muroc and the last souped-up "gow job" of the SCTA rumbled into silence, the first chapter of the incredible world to be known as hot rodding fell silent. Nearly four years of savagery across the globe would pass before the engines would again thunder with even greater power.

CHAPTER THREE
CALIFORNIA CAR MADNESS

Frank Livingstone, Jr. was barely a year old when his mother and father loaded him, his four year-old brother Arnold, and the family furniture into a sedan and a small truck to leave Springfield, Illinois, forever. They headed west in the summer of 1926 using the newly opened and much-celebrated Route 66, soon to be known as the "Mother Road" because of its ability to give birth to new opportunity on the dreamy, gold-paved streets of southern California. According to the mythology of the day, the sun shone forever in California, and everyone had a shot at movie stardom. But rather than seeking his fame and fortune on the Silver Screen, "Duke" Livingstone acquired employment with the rapidly growing school system in the eastern suburb of Pasadena. His wife, Lenore, known to everyone as "Toots," opened a beauty parlor, and the family settled into a classic, middle-class, Golden State good life.

Southern California vibrated with the rising thunder of the car culture. The streets of the vast urban complex swarmed with fast cars of all kinds, precursors of the hot rod and sports car movements that would seize the area following World War II. Legion Ascot, the wildly dangerous five-eighths-mile dirt track in the London Hills on the edge of Glendale, would produce great stars like Rex Mays, Ernie Triplett, and Al Gordon. In 1936, when Gordon and his riding mechanic, Spider Matlock, died in a gruesome crash that brought the Hearst newspapers to full cry, the deadly oval closed forever. Farther north, in the high desert beyond the dangerous Grapevine, Ridge Route, Angeles Crest Highway, and El Cajon passes, lay the dry lakes at El Mirage, Rosamond, and Muroc, where the pioneers of the great California hot-rod industry were running their modified roadsters and coupes on dusty summer weekends.

Young Frank Livingstone was raised in a normal, middle-class Pasadena household in a community better known for its annual Rose Bowl college football game than for any involvement with the booming automotive culture. He and his friends built wooden carts and rolled them down a nearby hill in mock Soap Box Derby competitions. They carved model airplanes and automobiles out of balsa wood and engaged in other simple boyish pleasures of the day, long before video games and remote-controlled models were in the minds of even the most daring futurists.

As Frank entered his early teen-age years, he helped his brother Arnold build a Soap Box Derby racer, which in those days required that the boys fabricate the car from scraps.

Their machine, steered by a rope tiller, was labeled the Gilmore Special, in honor of Gilmore Red Lion oil. The Los Angeles-based lubricant was owned by racing enthusiast Earl Gilmore, who had built Gilmore Stadium and sponsored cars that had won the Indianapolis 500 in 1935 and 1937. Although Arnold failed to be invited to the Derby finals held in Akron, Ohio, he and Frank were both awarded tin racing-style helmets of the type worn by Wilbur Shaw as he drove his Gilmore Red Lion Special to victory at Indianapolis in 1937.

In 1939, Gordon Babb, the owner of the Ace Model shop in Pasadena, hired Frank—now nicknamed "Duffy" for some forgotten reason—to refill bottles of dope used in those days to harden the surfaces of the balsa and paper wings used on model airplanes. He earned 75 cents per week. While his primary job was to serve customers building model airplanes, he spent his idle hours at the shop carving model cars and dreaming of the day when he would build himself a real hot rod.

Thanks to a model airplane engine purchased from Babb's shop in 1940, Duffy built a gas-powered race car and entered the world of "spindizzies." These tiny, gas-powered cars became popular in the late 1930s and were run on 60-foot tethers in crazed, high-speed circles. Livingstone competed with his car on the vast macadam expanse of the Rose Bowl parking lot.

That future had to wait until the completion of some ugly business against millions of men in the German Wehrmacht and the Japanese Imperial Army. Duffy graduated from

Longfellow Senior High School and attended John Muir Junior College with the understanding that the Armed Services lay ahead. In March 1942, he joined the Navy and, like tens of thousands of young men, was dragooned through boot camp in San Diego where he was in Squad 184—a number that would come to have a different meaning in his life in later years. After being briefly stationed in Jacksonville, Florida, in building 84, he was transferred to Panama for antisubmarine duty aboard ancient, but steadfast PBY twin-engine flying boats. He was assigned to Squadron 84 before heading to the South Pacific.

While the PBY's were designed strictly for patrol and rescue duty, the Navy soon discovered that they could be employed as dive bombers against slow merchant shipping as well. Incredibly, the old birds, theoretically limited to a maximum speed of 190 knots, were dived at 250 knots from 8,000 feet. They dropped a pair of 1,000 pound bombs, two 500 pounders and two 100 pound demolition bombs (developed in World War I) on freighters and barges supplying Japanese troops all over the South Pacific. Serving as Flight Captain, Airman Second Class, Livingstone would open one of the large, plexiglass bubble hatches midship on the PBY and toss out the 100 pounders.

During a five-week period in 1943, Livingstone's PBY squadron, painted flat black and flying night missions, sank 13,000 tons of enemy shipping and earned a rare and much honored "well done" from General Douglas Macarthur. The Squadron accounted for three percent of all Japanese shipping sunk in the Pacific.

The duty was harrowing and often bloody. Livingstone missed being hit by anti-aircraft fire by inches on several occasions, and during a wild attack on a 10,000-ton enemy freighter in the Celebese Islands, his Catalina was raked with 20-millimeter gun fire, knocking out the port engine and wounding several crewman. As the aged amphibian limped home across 550 miles of open ocean, its young navigator, who had been wounded in the crossfire, bled to death.

After another narrow escape in the Leyte Gulf when a Kamikaze landed within 30 feet of where he was standing on his seaplane tender's deck, Livingstone's two-year tour of constant combat was completed and he returned to the United States. While stationed at Los Alamedas Naval Station in California and awaiting yet another combat tour, the war mercifully ended and he went home to Pasadena to join the millions of jobless veterans suddenly pouring into the employment markets.

Duffy took a job at friend Dave Mitchell's welding shop in Eagle Rock, a few miles west of Pasadena. Knowing nothing about the art of arc welding, but well trained in Navy-style mechanics and naturally talented with tools, Livingstone was a quick learner and soon was using his new-found income to build a roadster—now commonly known among the California performance crowd as a "hot rod." Mitchell had sold him a 1932 Ford roaster soon to be known universally as a "Deuce" for $400. Having found a pre-war Cadillac V-8 in a junkyard, Livingstone shoe-horned the immense, heavy, low-revving-but-torquey old flathead into his new machine and joined the Stokers, a large, local hot rod club that ran regularly on the dry lakes at SCTA events. Livingstone competed at Muroc on a number of occasions with the Caddy hot rod, but set no records, running in the 110 mile-per-hour range. But Livingstone was less interested in raw, straight-line speed than in overall handling and performance. Driving over the twisty Angeles Crest highway on the way to the Lake was more challenging for him than the high-speed straight-line Muroc runs. He later observed, "Taking a curve at 120 miles an hour was a lot more interesting for me than running straight at that same speed."

In January of 1947, the Southern California Timing Association and other clubs organized a small roadster show at the Los Angeles National Guard Armory. Two young veterans working for a small motion picture promotion agency, Bob Petersen and Bob Lindsey, were assigned the job of selling booth space to area speed-equipment operators and speed shop owners. As a promotion piece, the pair scraped together a few short stories, a batch of photos, and a handful of advertisers and published a 24-page magazine they dared to call *Hot Rod*—mindful that the phrase was a hot button of controversy among the press and the general public.

The 25-cent-per-copy magazine sold out instantly and indicated to the pair that a massive potential market existed for a monthly magazine on the subject. Also realizing the possibilities were Wally Parks, who came aboard as editor, and cartoonist Tom Medley, who began penning his *Stroker McGurk* comic strip that chronicled the joys and foibles of the young sport. Advertisers included Ed Iskenderian's small camshaft business and Don Blair's Pasadena speed shop.

Within a decade, Petersen Publishing would, thanks to *Hot Rod*, *Motor Trend*, *Rod & Custom*, and other monthlies, rise to national prominence in the magazine publishing field and make Bob Petersen one of the richest men in America as well as a major supporter of the sport that he helped create.

By 1950, street racing, now called "drags," was underway everywhere, with thousands of hot rodders forming up *American Graffiti*-style at drive-ins across the LA basin. The Hearst newspapers, having long employed motorsports as a deadly shibboleth to boost circulation, began to screech in bold headlines about the "hot rod menace." The hot rodders responded by organizing drag races on vacant boulevards and avenues that would run all night, or at least until the police roared onto the scene and scattered the racers. At the same time, other restless veterans were forming outlaw motorcycle clubs, like the notorious Hells Angels and the Booze Fighters, to send further ripples of terror throughout the bungalows and new split-levels of the good burghers.

In an effort to ease the pressure by the media and law enforcement, Wally Parks became a leader in organizing the National Hot Rod Association, which began to sanction controlled drag racing on the several airport runways that dotted the area.

Led by veterans who had been exposed to high-powered machinery during the war and who were openly restless about a return to mundane civilian life, motorsports grew exponentially in the postwar years. In addition to the hot rod and motorcycle movements operating at full bore, another new and exotic aspect of the sport developed when veterans from the European theatre brought home prewar English MGs, Rileys, Aston-Martins, and Triumph roadsters. These sporty imports were soon to be followed by a flood of new MG-TC two-seaters that rolled off the Abington, Berkshire, assembly line beginning in October 1945, only months after the war ended. Even with a top speed of only 78 miles per hour, these agile little machines generated a whole new group of enthusiasts who would also embrace the svelte Jaguar XK120 that reached U.S. shores in 1950.

The sports car revolution was underway, triggered first by road races held in Watkins Glen, New York in October 1948, then spreading across the nation to the car-crazy West Coast. Intrigued by the superior handling of the British machines in comparison to the unwieldy, chrome-laden sedans being offered by Detroit, Livingstone bought a second-generation MG-TD in 1952. Even though a hardcore hot rodder still referred to foreign car devotees as "sporty car" types and "tea baggers," Livingston became increasingly interested in road racing competition that was being organized by the West-Coast-based California Sports Car Club and the East-Coast-based Sports Car Club of America.

As dry lakes racing expanded, Wally Parks' nascent National Hot Rod Association gained strength, and the sports car movement grew in popularity, a fourth arena for racing enthusiasts was also roaring at full throat. The California Roadster Association sanctioned oval-track events for hot-rodded roadsters. Between the CRA and the insanely popular West-Coast midget racing, nine of the ten winners of the Indianapolis 500 during the decade of the

1950s would have Southern Calfornia roots. Johnny Parsons, Troy Ruttman, Bill Vukovich, Bob Sweikert, Pat Flaherty, Sam Hanks, Jimmy Bryan, Jim Rathmann, and Rodger Ward all honed their skills in southern California roadster and midget competition in the late 1940s and rose to dominance in the 1950s in American championship competition.

Some of these new motorsports pursuits came together in unexpected ways, one example being an early confluence of the hot rod and sports car movements. In 1948, Los Angeles fabricator Willis Baldwin built a Ford-based, aluminum-bodied, sports car for Englishmen Phil Payne. He followed it up with another Baldwin Ford-powered hot rod/sports car special that set fast time in qualifying for the Palm Springs road races in 1949. The same year a trio of motorsports greats—Indy car builders and master craftsmen Emil Diedt and Lujie Lesovsky, plus Phil Remington, who was to become the key sidekick of Caroll Shelby on the Cobra projects— teamed up to build a beautiful sports-rod for sportsman Stirling Edwards. In 1952, the legendary father of "Ol Yeller," Max Balchowsky, arrived on the sports car scene with a Deuce highboy powered by a flathead LaSalle V-8 built by dry lakes and CRA racing star Yam Oka. A year later, Ak Miller built the first of two of his famed "Caballo de Hiero" (Iron Horse) hot rods that competed both in Mexico's Pan American Road Race and in Italy's Mille Miglia.

By the early 1950s, a rift had developed between the so-called "purists" loyal to thoroughbred European marques like the MG, Ferrari, Jaguar, Maserati, and Porsche and the

"American Iron" enthusiasts. The latter employed the Ford-Mercury 59A flathead V-8 and the new, overhead-valve, short-stroke V-8s from Cadillac and Chrysler to power their so-called "specials," like those pioneered by the likes of Baldwin and Edwards.

By 1950, an Anglo-American hot rod began to dominate the competition when London garage owner and Ford representative Sydney Allard exported to America his lightweight Allard J2 roadster—a long-nosed, cycle-fendered machine first offered with a Ford-Mercury flathead. This powerplant was utilized by Roy Richter, the owner of Bell Auto Parts and former hot rodder, midget racer, and possessor of two of the most famous names in motorsports, Cragar and Bell. On a whim, Richter used his freshly-minted J2 to win the main event on June 25, 1950, at the California Sports Car Club race held on the airfield and blimp base at Santa Ana. (This would also serve as the venue for early NHRA-sanctioned drag races.) Despite Richter's victory, the aged flatheads were deemed too weak and prone to overheating (some called them "hot water heaters") for serious competition. Many owners on both the East and West Coasts replaced them with the new 331-cubic-inch overhead-valve (OHV) Cadillac V-8, which developed a whopping 160 horsepower out of the box and could easily be modified to produce well over 300 horsepower. This engine turned the 1,800-pound Allard into a winner, despite its evil penchant for extreme oversteer.

Back in Detroit, Chrysler responded to the short-stroke V-8s from Cadillac and Oldsmobile by offering its legendary Hemi. By the following year, it was rated at a stock 210

Sept. 19th '54

Dear Brock ;

    I'm returning to you herewith four dollars, your dues for the '54 season were paid and ESTA has no emblem as yet. When you visit the Strip you can purchase a T shirt with Empire State Timing Assoc. silk screened on it. I'll leave it to you to get your own size shirt.

    Your new '55 ESTA Membership Card will be along soon - Will Hackett is the new Pres. and he has to sign them. You will also receive a Bulletin from your new Pres. shortly. Will is a fine guy and will work like the devil for us, I know he'll make a real good President.

    Guess I'd better tell you that I think your book is a real goodie or you'll think I can't read. Yes sir Brock, it is a very top book for young fellows and should assist the growth and interest in organized Hot Rodding a great deal. I wish you the best of success with it.

    Enough for now, hope to see you Draggin' next Sunday.

Yours sincerely,

Harry DeWaters.

Letter from NHRA:

In 1954, new NHRA members received personal letters.

Yates and friend Jim Berray attack the $15.00 32B.

A stock 59A Ford V-8 is installed.

The 32B would give way to the MG-TD as realities intervene.

Yates and his father, Raymond F. Yates, who triggered his enthusiasm for fast cars.

MG-TD: The seventy-odd tired horsepower had limitations.

Cal Club hot rod versus sports car. Jack McAfee, in John Edgar's 857S Ferrari, passes a spinning Max Balchowsky, in his famed "Ol' Yeller," at Palm Springs, November 1956. *Ken Parker, Edgar Motorsports Archive*

The elite of California sports car racing: John Edgar equipment at Palm Springs, 1956.
Lester Nehamkin, Edgar Motorsports Archive

(Type or Print)

OWNER: _____ DUFF   LIVINGSTONE _____

    Address: _____ 1590 LAS LUNAS _____ PASADENA CALIF. _

BUILDER: __ DUFF ____ Address: __ SAME _____

BODY: Make: _25_ _T_ _RDS._ Year: ____ Channeled? ____ How much? ____

    Chopped? _____ How much? _____ Paint: RED & WHITE _

INTERIOR: Upholstery: _____

    By whom? _____

    Instrument panel: _____

FRAME: _____ FRONT AXLE: _____

BRAKES: AIRCRAFT BENDIX & 53 LINCOLN _ SPINDLES: 40 FORD _

WHEELS: (type) FORD FRONT - MAG. REAR _ (size) _16_ ~ 15 _

TIRES: (front) 6.50 X 16 (rear) 8.20 x 15 SHOCKS HOUDAILLE -50-50

STEERING: 25 DODGE _____ TRANSMISSION: 58 CORVETT 4 SPEED

REAR END: HALIBRAND. CENTER SECTION (41 FORD) _ GEAR RATIO: _____

ENGINE: (year & make) 55 CHEV V8 _ Cubic in. 283 ____

    Stroke: STOCK _____ Relieved? _____ Bore: 1956 BORE _

    Valves ported? _____ Cam: E-2 ISKENDERIAN _____

    Head & compression ratio: 10-1 _____

    Intake manifold: EDELBROCK _ Carburetor: 97 - 3 ___

    Pistons: JAHNS HIGH DOME _ Flywheel: WEBER (make, type, how many)

    Ignition: SPALDING _____ Clutch: 11" POWER BUILT

EXHAUST SYSTEM: GP MUFFLER SERV. ~ MONROVIA _____

RADIATOR 46 FORD _____ SHELL: SPRINT CAR TYPE ____

BUMPERS: _____ HD. & TAIL LTS. _____

TOP SPEED: 125 MPH ___ HP: _____

    how calculated   how calculated

WEIGHT: 1325 (lbs) DRIVER COST: $2500.00 TIME TO BUILD: 1 YEAR

OTHER MODIFICATIONS: _____

— OVER —

Duffy's data sheet for the Eliminator that he prepared for Rod & Custom magazine in early 1959.

(Part two)

BACKGROUND OF OWNER: (include age, where born, family status, job,
                hobbies, community interests (clubs, churches, etc.), why did
                he built this car, any special problems and how overcome, etc.)

SPRINGFIELD ILL - JAN. 25 · 1925 ~ SINGLE - PARTNER OF GP MUFF.
& GO KART MFG. CO. INC. RACING - SKIN DIVING - GO KARTING.

CONVERTED TRACK ROADSTER TO SPORTS CAR.
WANTED TO RACE ROADSTER WITH SPORTS CARS

HAVE RACED WITH SCCA - CSCC - RRTA

        PALM SPRINGS - RIVERSIDE - POMONA - HOUR GLASS - WILLOW SPRING
PHOENIX - SANTA BARBARA. PARAMOUNT RANCH. SAN DIEGO.
HAVE PLACED 1ST OR 2ND IN LAST 5 RACES (C.MOD.)
                IN CLASS
PLACED 5TH IN OVER 2000 CC POMONA GRAND PRIX 11TH OVER ALL
QUALIFIED 19TH FASTEST OUT OF FIELD OF 52 CARS

SUGGESTIONS FOR FREE LANCE PHOTOGRAPHERS: Photos must be sharp, 8 x 10
                glossy. If photographer doesn't have enlarger send negatives. At
                least two photos should include owner of car—overall and closeup.
                Coverage should include: front, rear, both sides, 3/4 front left,
                3/4 front right, 3/4 rear left, 3/4 rear right, dash right and left
                sides, engine right and left sides.

                Camera should be on tripod for engine shots and at least two light
                sources should be used to give brilliant detail. Other photos should
                include closeups of any interesting detail or modification on car.
                Keep background uncluttered.

The Eliminator with its new Chevrolet small-block engine, 1956.

Duffy among the "tea baggers." The Lotus 11 is driven by Sammy Weiss.

The Eliminator often ran as a C-modified, complete with fenders and a spare tire.
Greg Sharp collection

Paramount Ranch, 1958. The Eliminator competes as a Formula libre car without fenders, headlights, spares, or other additions.

On the grid, Santa Barbara 1958, complete with his standard polka-dot helmet.
Lester Nehamkin

horsepower. This engine would be used by many sports car aficionados, including Briggs Cunningham who used Chrysler power in his beautiful C4 and C5 sports cars that almost won the Le Mans 24 Hour race on several forays in the mid-1950s.

This flood of ultra-fast Allards, Ferraris, and Jaguar C-Types from Europe and the availability of powerful engines from Detroit had, by 1952, created a sports car racing craze on both coasts. Enthusiast investors began to construct racing circuits carved out of rural farmland, and racing enthusiast General Curtis LeMay opened Air Force bases to organized competition.

Sports cars, hot rods, drag racing, dry lakes competition, midgets, and track roadsters were all soaring in significance as young veterans turned their restless, postwar interest toward high-powered automobiles of all kinds. As Detroit began to respond, first with engines and then, in 1953, with the first Corvette, a new speed equipment industry was rising up in southern California to form the foundations of the hot rod movement. Heading it were manifold and cylinder-head builder Vic Edelbrock; cam grinder Ed Iskenderian; ignition system gurus the Spalding brothers; Roy Richter and his steering wheels, helmets, and custom wheels; Ted Halibrand and his pioneering magnesium wheels, brakes, and differentials; Sandy Belond and his mufflers; and the list goes on. They were forging a new industry that would, by the end of the century, generate tens of billions of dollars annually.

In Van Nuys, a thriving suburb of Los Angeles, another speed-crazed young veteran named Jay Chamberlain had his own ideas about motorsports competition. A talented mechanic working at Austrian transplant Johnny Von Neumann's thriving imported car dealership on Ventura Boulevard in North Hollywood, Chamberlain raced midgets and planned to compete in the California Roadster Association circuit with a 1925 Model-T bucket roadster he was building in his garage. Circumstances would intervene that would send his career in an opposite direction, finally establishing him as a fine sports car driver and, more importantly, as the West Coast distributor of Colin Chapman's Lotus sports-racing and formula cars. Highly successful with Lotus 18 Formula Juniors and small sports-racers in the late 1950s, Chamberlain would enter seven Formula One races in Europe during 1962 with an independently financed Lotus-Climax, finishing as high as fifth at Goodwood.

A decade would pass before Chamberlain's international Formula One efforts however, and in 1952, he was hammering together his CRA roadster with plans to bang wheels with such future Indianapolis stars as Troy Ruttman, the Rathmann brothers Dick and Jim, Manuel Ayulo, and Jack McGrath.

His car would be based on a 1929 Ford frame found in a junkyard, applying a transverse leaf-spring suspension and 1928 Dodge passenger car steering. The only unique item on the car would be a hand-hammered nose and hood fabricated out of sheet steel (to handle the rigors of close-in track racing) by the genius fabricator Emil Diedt, a German expatriate whose exquisite bodies would grace numerous sports cars, Indianapolis cars, and all the famed Reventlow Scarabs.

As Chamberlain began to assemble bits for this roadster, word came that the CRA was abandoning rules requiring stock-based frames and would permit the use of tubular sprint-car-style chassis. These would be lighter and stiffer than the old Ford rails Chamberlain was planning to use. Since he was about to fabricate an instantly obsolete car, he abandoned his roadster project and put the pieces—frame, body, the Diedt nose, and hood—up for sale.

By 1953, Dave Mitchell had begun manufacturing high-performance mufflers, while Livingstone had been experimenting with mufflers packed with fiberglass to produce a throaty sound without a serious effect on performance. Having a newly-developed expertise in muffler design and fabrication, Livingstone left Mitchell and teamed up with old high school pal Roy Desbrow to form Duff and Roy's Muffler Shop. They rented a small garage behind a Richfield gas station on Pasadena's Colorado Avenue across from hot rod pioneer Don Blair's Speed Shop.

At the time, Blair was campaigning a CRA roadster for driver Dick McClung at Gardena and other area tracks, and Duffy became an informal member of the pit crew. It was during this time that he met Jay Chamberlain. By then, Duffy had sold his MG TD in order to buy a 1953 Ford pickup to support the new muffler business. But his interest in sports cars still percolated and reached full boil when Chamberlain offered Duffy the collection of pieces he had accumulated for his aborted CRA campaign. Duffy snapped them up for a few hundred dollars, knowing that another friend, Paul Parker, a plumber by trade and a serious hot rodder, owned what was called a "full-house" Mercury flat-head V-8 and was seeking a chassis. Parker agreed that his engine would be well suited for what Livingstone insisted on calling "sporty" car competition, and Livingstone, Parker, and Desbrow joined forces.

Parker would supply the engine and new parts, Livingstone would build the car, while Desbrow tended to the expanding muffler business and served as crewman at the races.

In late 1952, Livingstone drove his new Ford pickup to Chamberlain's Van Nuys garage where he loaded up the chassis, T-bucket body, and Emil Diedt's beautifully crafted nose and hauled them back to his Pasadena Muffler Shop.

Within months, one of California's most unforgettable hot rods would take shape.

CHAPTER FOUR
AN EAST COAST WANNABE

At roughly the same time Duffy Livingstone was lighting up his welding torch and preparing to build the Eliminator, I was 2,800 miles away, laboring on my own hot rod. I had purchased it for the princely sum of $15 dollars, a rumpled, engineless 1932 Ford five-window coupe. For another $200, my father helped me buy a rebuilt Ford flathead 59A V-8 block. My shop was the open backyard of my parent's home in the serene suburb of Carlisle Gardens on the edge of Lockport, New York. It was a General Motors town, the home of Harrison Radiator division, where the corporation's heating and cooling equipment were manufactured and where everyone of means drove either a Cadillac or a Buick.

My father, who did not consider himself part of the local establishment though he had close friends in the management of Harrison, had for years driven Buicks. Aboard one of these regal four doors, I had learned to drive, while sitting on his lap, long before I was old enough to obtain a license. He loved cars and used to talk at length about watching Ralph DePalma and Dario Resta duel on the immense, high-banked two-mile board Speedway in the Sheepshead Bay section of Brooklyn. Years after his death, I found in his effects a drawing he had made as a small boy celebrating Harry Grant's victory in the 1910 Vanderbilt Cup behind the wheel of his giant chain-drive Alco, "Black Bess." I came by my passion for cars honestly.

After the Depression had descended on the nation and after serving as the managing editor of *Popular Science*, composing a pioneering radio column for the *New York Herald Tribune*, and writing the first ever book about television in 1928, my father returned to his roots in upstate New York. He then embarked on a successful freelance writing career that lasted until he passed away in 1966.

He was an early customer for one of the hot new short-stroke V-8s that powered Oldsmobiles and abandoned his favored Buicks about the same time I got my driver's license. I immediately attempted to become king of Lockport's roads. This ended shortly after my first speeding ticket and a minor traffic accident. My father then traded the Olds for perhaps the slowest sedan in Christendom—a two-ton, four-door DeSoto powered by a flat-six and a flaccid three-speed automatic transmission—and effectively caused my banishment to the back of the pack in the local street racing league.

His interest in cars remained, and in 1952, he purchased

a neat little MG-TD. Its decent brakes and solid handling elevated me once again to the major leagues among my peers. The little car became my own transportation as my work slowly continued on the 1932 five window—a long and arduous task lacking both money and skill.

Even in those days, when the enthusiast world was split between hot rodders and sports car lovers—who waved at each other, cult-like on the highway—I divided my loyalties between the two groups, voraciously reading *Hot Rod* magazine each month plus the bible of sports cars, *Road & Track*, and the journal of oval racing, *Speed Age*.

Hot Rod was edited by Wally Parks, the paterfamilias of the entire movement, while future editor Ray Brock served on the staff, as did Tom Medley, the wonderful sketch artist who penned the *Stroker McGurk* cartoons, and photojournalists Eric Rickman and Bob D'Olivo. These five men were to become icons in the hot rod world, and their contributions are still celebrated even today, years after they departed the scene. Ironically, *Road & Track*'s future editor (1958) was himself a hot rodder. Dean Batchelor, one of the most honored journalists in the business, was, at the time, editor of the tiny *Hop Up* magazine. In 1949, he had teamed with Alex Xydias, the founder of the famed So-Cal Speed Shop, to campaign a streamliner at Bonneville that in 1952 ran over 210 miles per hour.

Inspired by the stories and photos of men writing and racing in faraway California, I dreamed of the day when I would race at Watkins Glen and power down the drag strip at Santa Ana, with my MG and my Deuce coupe respectively.

But learning came through hard lessons. While it was integral to the sports car mantra of the day to hate "Detroit Iron," the wheezy horsepower of the MG had its limitations when dealing with cars issued from the Motor City. One day, as I was demonstrating the alleged superiority of the MG's sophisticated European technology (which I, of course, failed to realize dated to the early 1930s) I engaged in a street race with a middle-aged man in a lumpy Dodge business coupe, powered by a flat-head six-cylinder. This was a car beneath contempt for true believers.

Oddly, the Dodge driver refused to be intimidated by my superior British sports car. He hung on my bumper through series of bends. I then decided to exhibit the nimbleness of the MG and braked hard for a tight right-hander and yanked hard on the wheel. At that moment, the driver's door, a tiny panel positioned with a crude latch, swung open and, as the car juddered to a halt, I found myself half-hanging out of the seat, saved from a pavement scuffing only by my death grip on the steering wheel.

I looked back to see the Dodge driver, who had stopped on the roadside after witnessing my farcical near-crash. He was slumped over his steering wheel, hysterical with laughter. After a moment, he recovered himself, gave me a jaunty wave, and drove off.

The much-reviled "Detroit Iron" of the day was hardly as pitiable as we anointed-ones believed. Not only were big Lincolns and Chryslers winning in the Mexican Road Race and NASCAR's fledging "Grand National" (later to become the Winston Cup), but Cadillac, Chrysler, and Oldsmobile V-

8s were powering Allards, Cunninghams, Cad-Healeys, and Kurtis 500 sports cars all over the nation to major victories.

Several years later, my father traded the MG for a black Jaguar XK-120 roadster, which I truly believed to be the fastest road car in upstate New York, if not the entire nation; that is until I engaged in another race on a four-mile straightaway against a hemi-powered Chrysler sedan. The top speed of the Jaguar was known to be 120 miles per hour, based on tests conducted on Belgium's Jabbeke highway during the development of the car. I knew in my heart that the Chrysler had no chance once the big cat stretched it's legs. Again, like the bout with the Dodge business coupe, the results defied logic. The Chrysler driver snubbed against the tail of the Jaguar and, flat-out for two miles, stayed with me until a stoplight ended the contest. Again, with a wave and a smile, he was gone, and I was left to puzzle about the alleged miracles bestowed upon the colonials by British craftsmen.

Only through dumb luck and God's grace, did I manage to not kill myself in the Jaguar. My father had fitted the car with Firestone racing tires, which in fact were grooved truck tires with a compound rivaling granite. After several harrowing spins—including a high-speed 360 on a damp, two-lane road that miraculously left me witlessly pin-wheeling between the guard rails without hitting anything—I learned to treat the car with respect even at the hint of rain. Following my graduation from college and my entry into the Navy, my father sold the Jaguar and regained his long-lost loyalty to Buicks.

In the meantime, work on the hot rod had bogged down. Cold chiseling the body away from the frame was a noisy and arduous job, and the only sign of progress was the purchase of a set of Belond exhaust headers and installation of the Mercury engine into the frame. My parents began to hear grumblings about the project from their suburban neighbors. Then my departure for college brought the project to a standstill.

Somehow, even after joining the National Hot Rod Association in 1954, my ardor for the Deuce coupe slowly died away, dampened by my lack of a shop, mechanical skill, and disposable income. Somehow, college fraternity life, a growing romance with my future first wife, and the prospect of Naval duty after graduation shoved the hot rod project onto a back burner. Finally, my father grew tired of the skeletal remains defiling his yard and told me that it must either be completed or sold. At that point, a young enthusiast named Dudley Smith purchased the chassis, body, and engine, and carried on the effort. I believe he later replaced the flathead with a small-block Chevy and finished the car, after which its history goes dark. Perhaps, somehow, somewhere, it remains a 32 Five-Window that is the pride and joy of a current devotee of the hobby.

My career then took a turn away from hot rods. After returning from four years in the Navy, I began freelance writing about cars, mainly for *Competition Press* (now *Autoweek*) in an outrageous column called "Brockbusters". I also wrote occasionally for *Road & Track* and its sister publication, *Car Life,* before David E. Davis, Jr. hired me in 1964. He had recently taken over as the editor of the struggling *Car and Driver*. My job was managing editor, despite the harsh fact that I could neither manage nor edit.

While in San Diego during my stint in the Navy, I got several sniffs of hot rodding, California style. On a weekend pass to visit the Paradise Mesa drag strip in nearby Chula Vista, I saw the great local "Bean Bandit" dragster run by Joaquin Arnett in action. His all-Latino team had taken the pejorative "Beaner," used to describe Mexicans, and turned it into one of the most famous names in early drag racing. The Bean Bandit team set numerous speed records with their flathead, Ford-powered machines, both front- and rear-engined, and exemplified the incredible innovative powers that erupted in California during that period.

That same year, I had spent a Saturday at Montgomery Airfield, North of San Diego watching a sports car race rather elegantly titled the "Fiesta Del Pacifico at San Diego." The Long Beach MG Car Club and the California Sports Car Club sponsored the race. Because most of the big names in West-Coast sports car racing were back east chasing what was then the National Championship of the rival Sports Car Club of America, the field was rather meager, lacking such stars as Carroll Shelby and Jack McAfee.

The races had originally been scheduled for the Torrey Pines course between the posh suburbs of Del Mar and La Jolla where the Cal-Club had run events since 1952 on a network of ocean-side roads built by the U.S. Army during World War II. By 1956, land values had escalated to a point where the San Diego Chamber of Commerce decided to transform the property into a championship golf course, and all motorsports were cancelled. In a last-hour move, the Cal-Club arranged for a race at Montgomery Airfield located eight miles southwest of Torrey Pines. The course required that the runways be closed to air traffic for the weekend. This would be the only occasion upon which the Field was employed for anything but general aviation.

Bill Murphy, a Los Angeles Buick dealer, won the main event in his new, envelope-bodied Kurtis-Kraft, powered by a fuel-injected Buick V-8. His main rival was Billy Krause, a young hotshot in a Jaguar D-type, with Ken Miles running third in Johnny von Neumann's 550 Porsche Spyder. Miles also won the Under-1500-cc race with his famed MG Special "Flying Shingle," while back in 15th, unnoticed by me or the other spectators lining the snow-fences, was a novice driver from Riverside in a 1600-cc Porsche 356 Production class roadster. Fifteen years later, he and I would team up to win the Cannonball Sea-to-Shining Sea Memorial Trophy Dash. His name is Daniel Sexton Gurney.

There was a truly vivid machine on hand that I had read about in the July 1953, issue of *Hot Rod* magazine. Its number was 184. Its craggy, high-mounted Model-T bucket body gave it an unmistakable profile. The name of its driver, Frank Livingstone, meant nothing to me at the time, but having a special affinity for hot rods, I watched it rumble and skid around the flat runways with fascination. In the program, it was listed as "Eliminator Special."

While in San Diego, I had traded the tired 1949 Buick sedan that had carried my first wife Sally and I westward from Officers Candidate school in Newport, Rhode Island, to California for a used MG-TF. The little red roadster gave me a limited entrée into the exclusive world of sports cars, yet my interest lay with the weird hot rod that stood out among the low-slung European machinery. Late in the day, the Eliminator barged onto the course to participate in a nine-lap "Formula Libre" mixed-bag event that included such diverse machinery as a 1950 Talbot-Lago 4.5-liter Grand Prix car, a rare 1948 Alfa-Romeo-powered Nardi-Danese (sold in March 2003 at the RM Amelia Island exotic car auction for $275,000) and a cluster of noisy, motorcycle-engined, 500-cc single-seaters. Its big Chevy engine blaring impudently, the Eliminator won easily.

Back on board the ship, I read in the *San Diego Union* on Monday that Livingstone had also won a short race on Sunday against large-displacement production cars like Corvettes and Mercedes-Benz 300 SL Gullwings.

Perhaps inspired by the racing at Montgomery Field, I engaged a fellow officer and his MG-TD on a race along Coronado's Silver Strand, during which my 1500-cc miracle from the Morris Garage spun a bearing. Unable to afford a repair, I traded the car for a used Volkswagen, which I kept for several years and used to transport my wife and baby son, Brock, Jr., back for further sea duty on the East Coast.

But the memory of the Eliminator remained stuffed in a cranny of my brain, to resurface again with another story in the July 1958, issue of *Hot Rod* magazine titled "A 'T' in Fast Company." The story, written by Eric Rickman, was about the Eliminator and how it had developed into a serious sports-racing car in the West-Coast competition, powered by a 283 Chevy V-8 and driven by a guy known as "Duffy" Livingstone. He would appear again in the August 1960 issue of the magazine, but this time as a star in the booming world of go-karting. Livingstone had abandoned sports car racing to build his own "Go-Kart" machines in Azuza and was a player at the top levels of the sport with karts powered by German-built, single-cylinder Puch engines.

By then, I was out of the Navy and struggling with a career in writing while trying to become a serious race driver with then-popular Formula Junior cars in East Coast competition. As I moved along my own path in motorsports, the memory of that crazy hot–rod, hammering around the sun-drenched runways of Montgomery Field in the summer of 1956, remained filed deep in my memory bank. Little did I dream that it would burst into my life, as noisy and impudent as ever, forty years later.

I was hardly the only one who recalled the exploits of Duffy Livingstone and the Eliminator. What follows is the recollection of Steve Earl, the founder and impresario of the world-famous Rolex Monterey Historic Races and an expert race driver, collector, and general automotive enthusiast:

"High school days in southern California during the fifties was, I reckon, about as good as it could get. We were always seeing some form of exotic car going down the roads—hot rods, customs, sports cars, race cars, what have you. I seemed to gravitate to the sports cars for some unknown reason and, along with some buddies, would go off to the road races whenever possible. Palm Springs, Pomona, and Santa Barbara were the favorites. The familiar names included Bill Murphy, John Von

Neumann, Max Balchowsky, Bill Krause, Ken Miles, Ritchie Ginther, and Frank Livingstone. There were Porches, Jaguars, Frazer-Nashes, Lotuses, OSCAs, an occasional Ferrari or Maserati, and some pretty slick specials. The local aircraft and film industries were home for some amazing craftsmen.

"I remember one trip to the Santa Barbara road races. Bill Murphy was driving his Kurtis-Buick. He had won the last three or four events and was the center of attention. Von Neumann had a 3.5-liter Ferrari, Bill Krause a D-Jaguar. There was a C-Jag, a Healy 100S, and the specials, headed by Chuck Porter's Mercedes 300 SLS—a real beauty—Dick Morgenson's (Ol' Yeller), which was not a beauty, plus the Parkinson and the Baldwin. When the flag dropped, Murphy pulled away, only to spin and give the lead to Krause and the D-Type. Livingstone spun too. Watching Murphy work his way up from the back of the field was something. The acceleration of the Kurtis-Buick out of the corners was overpowering. Midway through the race the order stood, D-Type, Kurtis, Parkinson, Ferrari, Morgenson. But here came Livingstone in the Eliminator. An amazing sight it was, this white and red T-bucket hot-rod special driven by a guy in a red and white polka dotted helmet passing the Von Neumann Ferrari and taking fourth place! It was great race and my lasting impression will be of Duffy Livingstone and the Eliminator. It was 'Big Dog' versus 'Polo.'

"You had to be there! It was the summer of 1956. We had our own hero now. Footnote: Bill Murphy won the

next day. Twenty years after I'd started the Rolex Monterey Historic Races, people would comment on how many cars the event had been responsible in reviving. I'd say, 'Wait until the 'Eliminator shows up.' And guess what? Brock came calling!"

CHAPTER FIVE
THE ELIMINATOR ARRIVES

Mid-1950s racing technology was ossified between 1930s verities and breakthrough technologies born during the war. Developments in light alloys, fabrication, and new design themes developed in the main by the aircraft industry were on the verge of revolutionizing the sport.

Frank Kurtis, for example, altered American racing car design in 1945 by creating his tubular chassis midgets that instantly obsoleted prewar, rail-frame versions. In faraway Modena, Italy, Enzo Ferrari was employing similar technologies for his new sports-racing and formula cars.

Ted Halibrand, a design genius with an aircraft industry background, developed light, strong magnesium wheels, disc brake calipers, and quick-change rear ends, while Stuart Hillborn utilized aircraft principals to create a cheap, efficient direct fuel-injection system. Breakthrough technologies in bearing surfaces, lighter steel alloys, fiberglass compounds, synthetic rubber, and bonding and fastening methods had all risen out of the war effort and were being used by race car designers both in America and Europe.

In 1951, a Jaguar C-type, equipped with aircraft-style disc brakes, won the Le Mans 24 Hour race. A year later, Frank Kurtis stunned Indianapolis with his first roadster, equipped with its Offenhauser engine offset to the left, a tubular chrome-moly chassis, Hillborn fuel-injection, Halibrand disc brakes and wheels, and an adjustable torsion-bar suspension.

Yet for all the advances at Le Mans and Indianapolis, aged concepts still flourished. Until the end of the decade, Enzo Ferrari resisted using magnesium wheels in place of classic wires, torsion-bars in place of leaf springs, or any notion of a mid-engine design long after Englishmen John Cooper and Colin Chapman had obsoleted his classic, front-engine Grand Prix cars.

At the far end of the technology spectrum, Duffy Livingstone, Roy Desbrow, and Paul Parker were constrained by available funds and had little choice but to build a sports-racing car that dated to the 1930s—rail frame, drum brakes, leaf springs, and flathead engine. Advances being made in Formula One, International sports car competition, and at Indianapolis were light years away from amateur southern California sports car racing, where a mixed bag of hot rod specials and a handful of exotic Ferraris, Maseratis, and Porsches were doing battle.

A few wealthy California players, including Johnny Von Neumann, Tony Paravanno, Roger Barlow, and John Edgar, as well as Briggs Cunningham in the east, had the financial power to buy or have built for them first-class racing machinery. Most enthusiasts, though, were left with the option of either purchasing a low-cost MG or Porsche Speedster and competing in production class races or, like Livingstone, Max Balchowsky, and transplanted Englishman Ken Miles, to name but three of many, to weld up their own "specials." Balchowsky would gain fame with his ragged, but fiendishly quick Buick-powered "Ol' Yellers," while Miles dominated the 1500-cc class with his brilliant, featherweight MG "Flying Shingle" specials.

Because of his hot rod background and muffler business, it was obvious that Livingstone would lean toward an American-based car. He purchased Jay Chamberlain's body and chassis, and Parker's engine was the only powerplant option, even though it was a borderline antique in the face of the new over-head-valve V-8s pouring out of Detroit and the appearance of powerful, overhead-camshaft engines from Europe.

Their budget was set at $2,500, meaning that junkyards would have to be prime sources of materials and serious ingenuity would have to be brought to bear on the project.

The first mission was to modify and strengthen Chamberlain's Ford frame rails, which Livingstone boxed for strength and drilled extensively for lightness. The frame was reinforced with cross members constructed of 4130 chrome-molybdenum steel—tons of which were now available as war surplus, making it the material of choice for American race car builders—and two roll-bars fore and aft of the cockpit.

The special used basic Ford Model-T transverse leaf-spring suspension with radius rods and the Houdaille friction shocks that were in wide use on oval track cars across the nation—as they had been since the mid-1930s.

Los Angeles was overloaded with so-called "war surplus stores" selling everything from leftover army blankets and bayonets to complete Allison aircraft engines at a fraction of their original cost. Livingstone hunted down one such store in West Covina, where he purchased, for a few dollars, a pair of aircraft bucket seats, some sheet aluminum, and two special Bendix brake shoes and backing plates, which he planned to mate with 1952 Lincoln drums and fit to the rear wheels of the hot rod. He also picked up an Army canteen that he would employ as a crankcase dump can, required by the California Sports Car Club rules.

As he was leaving, he spotted a 1940 Ford V-8 60 tubular axle half buried in the store's yard. "How much does that cost?' he asked the owner, knowing such a strong, lightweight unit was a rare item. "Aw, take it along," said the owner. "If you ever sell it, give me half the money." Livingstone agreed. The axle would never be resold, but rather stay with the car he was building throughout its nearly half-century-long odyssey.

The T-Bucket body required some ingenious modifications. Cal Club racing rules mandated that a driver's door be capable of being opened, presumably for safety reasons. Henry's "T" roadster had only one door on the right side of the body. This required that Duffy weld the right door shut and refit another to the driver's side after torching out an opening and fitting a second Ford door, complete with household hinges and a screen-door latch purchased at a local hardware store. This would create the only left-hand door Model-T roadster in the world and would prompt numerous questions about how and why the car was built. Livingstone developed a series of droll answers to such queries, perhaps topped several years later when a curious observer asked, "Where did this body come from? I've never seen one like it."

Never breaking a smile, Livingstone replied, "It's an early Corvette prototype body, built in 1925. Very rare."

Amazed at the revelation, the onlooker drifted away, having seen what he believed to be an extraordinary example of automotive design.

During the spring of 1953, *Hot Rod* magazine got wind of the project and editor Wally Parks dispatched his managing editor, W.G. "Racer" Brown, and photo editor, Eric Rickman, from their Hollywood Boulevard office to record the construction of the new sports-rod.

A story on the car, with pictures by Rickman and staff photographer Felix Zelenka, appeared in the June issue of the magazine, detailing how the car was fabricated and made ready for its first race at Palm Springs in March of that year.

Once the chassis and suspension were finished (complete with a Japanese army helmet, salvaged by Duffy in the South Pacific, that had been sawed in half and installed to serve as a pair of air ducts for the front brakes), Parker's donated Mercury V-8 was set in the chassis, coupled to a 1939 Ford three-speed gearbox with Lincoln Zephyr gears that offered wider second gear ratios for open road use. The engine had been "built up," as it was then called, by Darryl "Tim" Timmerman's Precision Rebuilding

Shop in Pasadena. Parker's 1942 Mercury flathead had been bored and stroked to 304 cubic inches with Evans aluminum heads, a Potvin "Eliminator" camshaft (hence the origin of the car's name), and a custom intake manifold mounting four Stromberg 97 carburetors.

Because it was to compete as a sports car, the Eliminator carried fenders. The rear pair was fabricated out of 1936 Ford roadster spare-tire covers, the fronts from 1931 Model-A rear fenders. A small mounting bracket was made for the rear trunk lid to carry the required spare-tire, and headlights were mounted on the fabricated front shock mounts that had also been drilled for lightness. The car was originally painted black, then overlaid with a coat of white primer that produced a sickly light pink hue in the California sunlight. It initially carried the number 102B , which had been assigned by the California Sports Car Club. Livingstone had requested 84 based on his long contact with that number, but had been told that all large-displacement cars had to carry three-digit numbers.

It weighed 1,760 pounds as it was prepared to enter its first race at the Palm Springs airport on the weekend of March 23, 1953. Parker, who was known around the shop as the "Animal," wanted to drive, as did Duffy. It was agreed that they would share time behind the wheel over the weekend, presuming they could get the car through the Cal Club's technical inspection process, where hot rods were not welcomed.

Livingstone and the crew flat-towed the Eliminator to the race behind their 1929 Model A stake-bed pickup, which would be employed for such work during the car's career. As would happen many times in the future, even with the flathead Ford V-8 Livingstone had installed in the Model A, it failed on the steady climb to the high desert. On several steep grades, the Eliminator was fired up and used to push the rig to the top.

Parker quickly justified his "Animal" nickname on the track, showing little subtlety or skill in handling the car, while Duffy quickly adapted to the sport. Worse yet, Paul Parker was simply too big to fit in the cockpit. A plumber by trade, he was built like an NFL lineman, and fully capable of manhandling a cast-iron bathtub into position by himself. Though an advantage in his chosen line of work, his size was a handicap while trying to wedge himself into the cramped cockpit of the Eliminator.

An English enthusiast named Harry Steel had commissioned Duffy and Roy to fabricate a set of exhaust headers for his Lincoln-V-8-powered J2 Allard. During the course of the project, he asked Livingstone to drive the car at Palm Springs. However, Steel and the Allard, while officially entered, never appeared, and Livingstone was left to concentrate on preparing his own car.

It was common practice in those days that almost anyone over 21 could climb into a car and race. Although Duffy had competed on the dry lakes, he had no experience in road racing, yet he and Parker were both permitted to drive. Later, as speeds increased and the competition became keener and more dangerous, driver's schools, novice races, and other training became mandatory.

During practice, clutch slippage immediately became a problem due to heat buildup. Livingstone tried to correct this by removing the cover plate from the top of the bell housing and installing a length of 3-inch diameter exhaust pipe to a point where it served as an air intake above the cowling.

Having already had numerous run-ins with what he was calling the "tea baggers," Livingstone knew that they could be easily tweaked. Once the clutch air intake was installed, he began to cover it while the car was in the pits, causing various club officials to believe it was a secret device to add engine power. Other competitors protested the strange outcropping capped with a carburetor air scoop, but Livingston refused to reveal its rather simple function, and the car carried it for several seasons.

Despite the ingenious clutch modification, the aged Ford transmission could not stand the beating and, during practice, gave up for the weekend. The team returned home having learned: (1) the car handled badly, (2) Parker was not a driver, and (3) a stronger gearbox and clutch was necessary if racing was to continue.

The debut of the car that Racer Brown referred to in his *Hot Rod* story as a "poor man's Cunningham" was less than auspicious. But few understood the competitive nature of Duffy Livingstone and his skills as a creative mechanic and intuitive engineer.

CHAPTER SIX
THE GO-KART IS BORN

The debut of the Livingstone-Parker-Desbrow Eliminator special at Palm Springs road races in March 1953 had hardly jiggled the needle among the true believers—just another home-built antique posing no threat to serious racers. Ex-sprint car driver and hot rodder Jack McAfee won the main event at the wheel of wealthy sportsman John Edgar's powerful Tipo 340 Ferrari. It was followed by another pair of 212s from Maranello. Hollywood sports car dealer Johnny von Neumann won the under-1500-cc class (in those days, simple rules split the competing cars between production and modified cars, over and under 1.5 liters) in a Porsche Le Mans coupe. The class would be hotly contested during the season by a mob of Porsches, Italian OSCAs, and Ken Miles superbly engineered, featherweight "Flying Shingle" MG special.

The Livingstone-led team ran only once more during the year, with Paul Parker driving unsuccessfully in a small race organized by the Long Beach MG Car Club held at Terminal Island Navy Base. The muffler business was growing rapidly for Duff and Roy, and a major expansion effort was being exerted, resulting in three stores opening in West Covina, Riverside, and Monrovia. Duffy had developed a muffler packed with fiberglass and had begun marketing "GP Mufflers," a pun on the shared acronym of "Grand Prix" and "Glass Pack," that produced excellent income and pushed thoughts of campaigning the hot rod further into the background.

The team returned to Palm Springs in January of 1954 with the Ford transmission having been replaced by a 1942 Cadillac-LaSalle three-speed—a unit Livingstone had used in his first hot rod, which he had purchased from Dave Mitchell. Not only was the Caddy stronger than the Ford, but it offered a taller second gear more flexible for use in mid-speed, 50–80 mile-per-hour corners that were common in road racing. Again, the car failed to finish and was returned to Pasadena where it sat until the Fourth of July. It was then taken to the Torrey Pines road courses on the edge of San Diego's posh La Jolla suburb where Parker practiced with insufficient success to even appear in the official results.

Finally, the car enjoyed its first hint of potential at the Santa Barbara airport course on September 5th when Duffy finished second in a 10-lap qualifying race, beating a strong field that included several Jaguars and Allards. But more mechanical woes kept it out of Sunday's feature race and the disappointment continued.

Nineteen fifty-five would be remembered as the year of doom: the Le Mans disaster that killed 88 spectators, and the deaths of ex-world champion Alberto Ascari, two-time Indy-500 winner Bill Vukovich, movie idle James Dean, and Indy stars Mike Nazaruk, Jack McGrath, and Manuel Ayulo. Due to the carnage, the American Automobile Association divested itself of its race sanctioning, and motorsports were outlawed in Switzerland and on most public roads across America.

However, at the same time, Detroit was entering what was to be known as the "horsepower race" with a series of high-performance cars that would shake the automotive world to its core. Leading the charge would be General Motor's top sales division, Chevrolet. In 1955, Chevy introduced a masterpiece of engineering, a V-8 engine that was smaller, lighter, and vastly more powerful than anything heretofore imagined. With a displacement of 265 cubic inches, the so-called "small-block" Chevy was offered in both sedans and the Corvette sports car, with optional outputs of up to 225 horsepower.

This engine, which is still in production with radical updates, is considered one of the greatest designs in history and has been used in countless racing applications for almost half a century. Thanks to the new V-8, Chevrolet sales exploded and the Corvette, which had been lagging behind Ford's V-8-powered Thunderbird, came alive. The new engine, with a revolutionary, lightweight, pushrod drivetrain that allowed revving past 7000 rpm— a figure unheard of in mass-produced powerplants up until that time—became an instant favorite with the racing crowd, although they remained in short supply on the aftermarket.

With Chevy's V-8 being unavailable to Livingstone and his team, they had little or no success throughout the 1955 season of seven more races. The car's entries at Santa Barbara, Palm Springs, Torrey Pines, and on a small course at Hansen Dam produced little satisfaction, although the Cal Club did relent and give Livingstone a permanent number: 184. He had requested 84, based on its connection to his Navy career, but the Club continued to mandate that all cars over 1500 cc had to carry a three-digit number, which prompted Livingstone to merely add a "one" to his request.

Other than the adaptation of the number and Paul Parker's retirement from the team due to his new marriage, there was little change in the "Duff and Roy's Muffler Shop Eliminator-Mercury," as the car was designated. During the final race of the season on December 4th at Palm Springs, the car finished 15th overall and 12th in the big-engine class in the Saturday preliminary but did not start in the Sunday main event. Clearly the old car had to be updated or sent into permanent retirement.

The Mercury was given one more chance in May 1956. Duffy hauled it 500 miles east for a regional sports car race organized in the backwater town of Wilcox, Arizona, one hundred miles east of Tucson in the Sulphur Springs Valley. There, the tired Merc breathed its last, blowing up in practice.

If the old car was to ever race again, another engine would have to be cradled in its 35-year-old frame rails. Otherwise, like the millions of Model-T's that preceded it, a rusty death would await it in a nearby junkyard. Livingstone understood that if the Eliminator was to have any chance

fun on wheels — for everyone!

The Go-Kart name that became generic for an entirely new class of motor vehicles.

Duffy races Dick Morgenson driving his Ferrari 250TR in Santa Barbara in 1959. These cars would be reunited at Monterey 38 years later. *George Robitschek*

Duffy carried his trusty Air Force gun camera in most of the 1959 races. The Maserati 200S is driven by Bill Nixon. *Bill Norcross*

Manhandling the Eliminator at Santa Barbara, 1959. The Go-Kart logo was added to the hood.
Bob Tronolone

Duffy clears the bridge at the L.A. Examiner Grand Prix at Pomona in 1959.

Through the tight stuff, Santa Barbara 1959.

Willow Springs hill climb, June 1958. First place in the big-car class.

Rounding the hanger at Santa Barbara, 1959. Ken Miles leads in the Porsche RSK followed by Don Hulette's Jaguar special. Dick Morgenson's Ferrari, Duffy, and Ak Miller in his Devin Olds follow behind. *Allen R. Kuhn*

Through the esses. Santa Barbara, 1958

The car as it surfaced in Tucson, Arizona, at Gordon Hall's home.

The origins of the second flathead Ford are a mystery.

The car arrived in from Chuck Porter's Los Angeles shop basically intact, but with a Ford flathead. The engine is the only remaining puzzle in the history of the car.

Gordon Hall, (center) sells the Eliminator to Phoenix lawyer and friend Tom Murphy (left) in the autumn of 1988. *Tom Murphy*

FOR SALE — Vintage dirt Track-T or run as vintage sports car, documented from 50s Pomona event with 265 Chevy engine. Halibrand quicky, rear wheels, flat head and spares. $8,000 or best offer. Jeff (602) 299-6714. Tucson.

Jeff Gamble's ad in National Speed Sport News' July 1988 issue that resulted in the Hall-Murphy transfer.

The first of two ill-fated Go-Kart attempts to run at Indianapolis with the Ollie Prather Kurtis-Kraft roadster. Bill Homier tried first, then Eddie Russo. *Indianapolis Motor Speedway*

The Eliminator as found in a Fullerton, California, storage shed and purchased by Brock Yates in early 1997.

against the increasingly faster Italian machinery and the new, space-framed California specials coming from shops like Troutman and Barnes with new Chevrolet V-8 power, a radical update of his aged iron would be imperative.

The first move was to dump Parker's old Mercury flathead and replace it with one of the revolutionary small-block, 265-cubic-inch Chevy V-8s. Unable to buy a new one, Livingstone sought out a speed shop in Los Angeles owning a small supply of early 1956 models that had been scrapped under a dealer warranty program. They had theoretically been destroyed by punching holes in the block, cracking the piston skirts, and burring the ends of the crankshaft, all of which could easily be repaired by hot rodders like Livingstone. He returned to Pasadena with an engine, after parting with $50. Another $30 obtained a set of truck cylinder heads with larger valves. Darryl "Tim" Timmerman, who had built up Parker's flathead, took over the Chevy rebuilding project and quickly repaired the block, re-bored the cylinders to 283 cubic inches, and inserted lightweight Jahns Pistons and a radical Iskenderian E3 camshaft. When finished, the freshened Chevy was estimated to produce well over 300 horsepower. They coupled it with Livingstone's old Cadillac-LaSalle three-speed transmission, there being no domestic 4-speed gear-boxes on the market (the Borg-Warner T-10 Corvette box was a year away).

The ancient Ford rear suspension and differential had to be updated. Because Livingstone was old friends with Frank Kurtis and his employees in nearby Glendale, he took the Indianapolis car builder's advice and converted the rear suspension to torsion bars, which were all the rage at the

Speedway. Duffy also chose a Halibrand quick-change rear-end, which offered both strength and reliability plus the ability to make final-drive gear changes depending on track length and conditions.

A new set of exhaust headers, using the inner drive shafts from a pair of 1936 Fords, were fabricated in Duff and Roy's shop, where final assembly of the car was completed in mid-1956. An early debut took place at the afore-mentioned Montgomery Field event I witnessed in San Diego.

It was immediately clear that the torsion bar suspension was not working. Despite endless fiddling with the setup by Duffy, Desbrow, and a crew that generally included Vern Taylor, Duffy's father, Duke, and another lifelong friend of Duffy's, Paul Vandervere, better known as "Mooch," the car was a cranky beast around the corners, alternating between radical oversteer and unpredictable understeer.

Livingstone began to doodle plans for a new car; not a rail-frame antique like the Eliminator but rather a space-frame sports car with a full aluminum body; one that would resemble the type being built in England by the likes of Brian Lister and be inspired by advanced, monocoque concepts used by Jaguar on their Le Mans-winning D-types.

Livingstone often consulted with a long-time friend named Art Ingels, who was one of Frank Kurtis' key employees and a fine race car fabricator in his own right. In 1956, he was poking around Ingels' shop when he spotted a toy-like vehicle parked on the workbench. It was the essence of rudimentary; four wheels on a rectangular 4130 chrome-moly frame with a two-cycle West Bend Model 750 lawnmower engine mounted on the back. No suspension. No gearbox. No body. "What's that thing?" Livingstone asked Ingels, "It's pretty damn cool," .

"Just something I've been fooling with. Kind of a cart thing I built with one of Frank's leftover lawnmower engines," answered Ingels.

He explained that during a complex legal wrangle between Kurtis and the McCulloch Company—the maker of West Bend products—the lawnmower powerplants had been offered to Kurtis-Kraft employees for $25 each. Ingels had purchased one and welded up what he called his "little car." Although he was a large man, weighing 210 pounds, Ingels told Livingstone that his 80-pound machine was capable of hauling him around at over 30 miles per hour.

Instead, it was Ingel's boss, Frank Kurtis who was given the shot at building more "little cars." But the master craftsman was too wrapped up with his Indianapolis roadsters and his 500 series sports cars, as well as his personal favorite, tiny, kid-sized quarter midgets, to take on the project. He would later enter the field with a Kurtis Kart, but it was too late and the car failed to make a dent in the burgeoning market.

Intrigued by the idea of a miniature car that would carry a full-sized man at such speeds, Livingstone asked Ingels if he could buy one of the West Bends and build a so-called "little car" for himself. Ingels agreed, understanding that if a few more were built, perhaps some informal racing could be organized in a nearby parking lot.

Livingstone rushed back to his GP muffler shop, now relocated and expanded in Monrovia, and began using his tube-bending equipment to fabricate one of the machines that he had designed on a paper bag.

His pal, Dick Vandevere, AKA "Mooch" due to his endless habit of smoking other people's cigarettes, came by the shop and spotted the project. "Hey, build me one," he proclaimed.

"I'll do you a deal," said Livingstone to Vendevere, who was an auto parts salesman and toured the Los Angeles basin. "We need wheels, bearings, chains, a sprocket—stuff like that. You get the pieces and I'll build the cars." (They were not yet called karts.) A deal was struck, much like the one he had made with Paul Parker when the Eliminator had been built.

Before the two little machines were finished, another friend, Tom Noel, known as "Rancho Randy," spotted the project and ordered a third. He was running the DeAnza Muffler Shop in Riverside for Livingstone and Desbrow and was an integral part of the operation. Then Desbrow became intrigued with the little cars and a fourth was laid down, thanks to Livingstone's welding skills, which at the time had reached a high art.

Within weeks, Art Ingels notion for a tiny, lawnmower-powered, four-wheeler that would haul around a grown man at high speed (relatively speaking) had blossomed into a tiny trend in east Los Angeles. An explosion in interest began that was to spread around the world and alter the state of automobile racing forever.

The first outing for these elemental machines was in the parking lot of the Rose Bowl stadium where teen-ager Livingstone had run model airplane-powered cars before

World War II. The impudent sound and curious sight of these miniature machines hauling grown men around in circles soon attracted small crowds. Dozens of others soon joined in, bringing their "little cars" with different power-plants, but still retaining the truncated 80-inch wheelbase that would form the essence of the class.

As the number of players increased, Livingstone suggested that rubber cones be laid out to form a road course. Soon informal races where being organized and crowds of the curious increased to a point where the Rose Bowl authorities became alarmed about liability issues and summarily ejected the fledging racers from the property.

Earl Pfost was a young patrol on the Pasadena police force when the first karters appeared on the east Area K parking lot of the Rose Bowl. He remembered the repeated calls from neighbors complaining about the insect-like buzzing issued from the miniature machines as they circled at ever-increasing velocities. However, the calls generated a friendship between Pfost and Duffy that led to him watching the Eliminator race on several occasions and finally to his own participation in the karting world.

At that point, an enthusiast named Don Bobenick, who would rise to prominence in the nascent movement, arranged with a shopping center in West Covina that closed on Sundays to permit racing on its large parking lot. Within months, Ingels' pioneer machine exploded into yet another iteration of motorsports rising out of southern California.

Duffy Livingstone instantly grasped the potential. He and Desbrow partnered with war surplus dealer Bill Rowles—

who could source all kinds of materials—and decided that manufacturing the little machines offered more potential than the muffler business. They set out to convert their Monrovia shop. But what to call their products? At that time, Lynn Wineland, the art director of *Rod and Custom,* a small, Los Angeles-based enthusiast monthly, was moonlighting as the creator of GP muffler advertising.

During a planning session, it was Wineland who suggested the new product be called a "Go-Kart." The name was copyrighted and Go-Kart manufacturing was formed. Limited production began with a basic Go-Kart selling for $129, ready to race. The name would become synonymous with an entire class of automobiles around the world thanks to Lynn Wineland. Spencer Murray and Marvin Patchen, the editor and managing editor, respectively, of *Rod and Custom,* were the first two Go-Kart customers as their magazine became a fevered supporter of the new sport.

By 1957, the karting craze had spread across southern California and was creeping eastward, soon to engulf the nation. Ingels had started his own brand, called Caretta, while other manufacturers were sprouting up to feed off the new enthusiasm.

Bobenick, Livingstone, Patchen, Murray, et al, formed the Go-Kart Club of America in December 1957, wherein the rules relating to technical specification, classes, racing, and policies were set in place.

The Go-Kart business overwhelmed Duffy, Desbrow, and Rowles. Plans were offered for $25 each—a hefty sum in the mid-1950s. Yet each day, mail containing hundreds, sometimes thousands, of requests landed on their doorstep. A larger factory was located and the business expanded into a building on Irwindale Avenue in Azuza, where production boomed. Needing more space, the partners purchased land at 6300 North Irwindale Avenue in Azuza and constructed a 10,000 square-foot Butler building to manufacture both Go-Karts and a new product called a Mini-Bike. The "Big Bear Scrambler," weighing 50 pounds and powered by a 3.5-horsepower West Bend engine, sold for $149. Like the Go-Kart, it was not only an immediate hit, but it also instantly spawned imitators.

The little factory soon employed over 20 workers and ran two shifts to keep up with the demand. Livingstone, being the craftsman of the trio, looked after production while Desbrow handled the administration. Rowles, a natural extrovert, served as the front man and chief salesman. Being novices in business, especially one that offered so much potential for growth, little was done in terms of patent or trademark protection. This opened the door to a mass of competitors that would ultimately flood the market and would lead to the Go-Kart manufacturing company's demise.

In the midst of the madness, thoughts of racing the Eliminator, even with its fresh Chevy V-8, were by necessity placed on the back burner. Two of the GP mufflers shops were sold in order to concentrate on the karting business and plans for a special, dedicated racetrack for karts were formulated. A year later, Livingstone obtained the adjacent open land and built a tight, corkscrew-shaped, 11-turn half-mile road course strictly for kart racing.

Earl Pfost, who had first met Livingstone while a member of the Pasadena police force patrolling the karter's early forays at the Rose Bowl, later became a security guard at the Azuza track on the alternate Sundays when racing took place. Rather than monetary payments for his off-duty work, Pfost received a Go-Kart for his efforts and began racing as well. Now in retirement, he recalled the day when Dan Gurney appeared at the track and was given a few laps. "Although he had never been on a Go-Kart and never seen the track, he ran faster than I ever could within a few laps. Damn, that made me feel lousy," he mused.

The incredible new world of karting was about to lead Duffy Livingstone on an entire new path in motorsports, one that would carry the Eliminator to its greatest triumphs.

CHAPTER SEVEN
TIME MARCHES ON

The 1950s were a glorious decade for automobile racing. Regardless of the dangers imposed on the drivers, which bordered on insanely lethal, the energy, creativity, and general over-the-top variety of machinery that took to tracks around the world will remain a source of delight for enthusiasts for years to come.

Esthetics created a vast tapestry, ranging from the masterpieces hammered out by Italian coachmakers to the outrageous and the bizarre issues from the likes of George Barris, "Big Daddy" Roth, and other Dadaists in the California custom car world. Racing cars, regardless of their type, were sleek-lined and soft-edged, represented by Kurtis and Watson Indianapolis roadsters, lovely Costin-bodied Vanwall GP cars, and eye-popping beauties from Ferrari and Maserati.

No one knew the real truth about what made automobiles go fast. Aerodynamics, other than simple streamlining, were unknown. All manner of engines—supercharged, turbocharged, and normally aspirated—were tried. Everything from hunky Meyer-Drake four-cylinders to V12s from Ferrari to air-cooled, flat-fours from Porsche and in-line eights from Mercedes-Benz found their way to the tracks. Then came the muscular V-8s from Detroit to challenge the best of Europe.

Englishmen John Cooper and Colin Chapman experimented with mid-engine chassis, but such designs were by no means universally accepted as the solution. Nor did anyone have a full grip on the nuances of the fully independent wishbone suspensions that would revolutionize design a decade hence. The modern, ground-effects, mid-engine monocoque was not even in the haziest dreams of the most gifted designer-engineer on earth.

In a broad *Alice in Wonderland* sense, nobody knew anything.

Better yet, the high-dollar, sponsor-driven commerce and television exposure that would ultimately drive costs into the stratosphere were yet to become a reality. In European as well as American racing, sponsorship was limited to a few trackside banners and the occasional Mobil Flying Horse logo. Grand Prix cars carried no sponsorship whatsoever and, even at Indianapolis, signage was limited to a simple "Special" logo on the hoods and a few tiny decals from Champion Spark Plugs, Perfect Circle Piston Rings, and a few other regular supporters.

By the middle 1950s, southern California was awash in fast cars of every conceivable type. While the midget-racing craze had died away as well as the CRA roadsters, the dry lakes crowd of the 1930s and 40s had, for the most part, transferred their enthusiasms to NHRA-style drag racing. There, brilliant, self-taught designers and drivers like Mickey Thompson, who developed the "slingshot" dragster, and Floridian Don "Big Daddy" Garlits were revolutionizing the sport.

However, the star quality, the glitz and glamour, was centered on the sports car racing that had spread up and down the West Coast like a runaway virus. Racetracks were built at Riverside, Paramount Ranch, Willow Springs, and Laguna Seca, replacing the temporary open road circuits like those at Torrey Pines and Pebble Beach. Most open road circuits had been either deemed unsafe or plowed under, like the board tracks of the 1920s, lost to the fevered demands of the real estate market.

The movie colony had taken to sports car racing with a passion. Clark Gable was a regular attendee, while young superstar James Dean showed real talent behind the wheel of his Porsche Speedster until he was killed driving his new 550 Spyder on the way to a race in Salinas, California. International playboy Porfirio Rubirosa occasionally competed, albeit slowly, with his Ferrari in various races while squiring actress Zsa Zsa Gabor though the pits. Also on the scene was comedian Keenan Wynn and young Lance Reventlow, the son of billionaire Woolworth heiress Barbara Hutton (who had also had a brief marriage to Rubirosa).

Reventlow soon gathered up an elite team of California hot rodders, Indianapolis fabricators, and sports car experts to create his beautiful and grandly ambitious Scarab racecars.

Beyond the tracks, members of the movie colony, who had scooped up the hundreds of Ferraris, Maseratis, Porsches, Jaguars, and Mercedes-Benz sports cars, showed off on twisty Mulholland Drive in the Santa Monica Mountains north of Hollywood. On the flats below, the drive-ins swarmed with hot-rodders ready to street race for money and "pink slips" (registrations) on a moment's challenge.

"Cruising" the boulevards became a way of life for hot rodders, immortalized in George Lucas' brilliant *American Graffiti*. Drive-ins across the Los Angeles basin became famous hangouts. The El Monte In-N-Out on Valley, Farmer Boys on Colorado, Bob's in Glendale, and Henry's in Arcadia were but a few of the better known drive-ins where hot cars gathered every night of the week, year in and year out, and from which countless Beach Boys songs were inspired.

Everywhere across the great Los Angeles basin, from the steamy San Fernando Valley on the north to Newport Beach 50 miles to the south, hot cars roamed the streets and the growing network of freeways. Race shops and speed equipment manufacturers blossomed by the hundreds while great racing drivers like Rodger Ward, Bill Vukovich, Jimmy Bryan, Sam Hanks, Jim Rathman, and Bob Sweikert dominated Indianapolis. Young California lions like Phil Hill, Dan Gurney, Masten Gregory, and Richie Ginther at the same time were about to make waves in European Grand Prix and sports car racing.

There being little sponsorship involvement and virtually no television, financial stakes were at a minimum. Sports car racing was relatively pure, with a strict amateur code being enforced, although pressures for professional events would become overwhelming by the end of the decade. Wealthy men like John Edgar—a wild, hard-drinking sportsman whose family fortune came from the Ohio-based Hobart Company that manufactured food service machinery and Kitchen-Aid dish-washers—as well as East Coast gentleman racer Briggs Cunningham participated in motor racing purely on an amateur basis. Both the Cal Club and the Sports Car Club of America had strict policies against prize money, although professionalism in the form of sub-rosa payments to drivers and background help from manufac-turers was seeping into the sport. This was especially true at Sebring, Florida, where the annual 12-Hour endurance race brought European professional teams into direct competi-tion with American amateurs.

Regardless of the financial aspects of the sport, motor racing in the 1950s was undertaken at all levels with an amazing *joi de vivre*! Even at the top levels in Grand Prix competition and on the Indianapolis championship circuit, a hell-bent love of competition far transcended any riches to be found in the sport. Bill Vukovich, who many believe to have been the greatest of the Indianapolis drivers in the early 1950s—he won two 500s in a row, 1953–54, and died while heading for his third victory in 1955—bought a modest gas station in his native Fresno with his winnings, such as they were.

Race drivers of the era were pure adventurers, prepared to face almost certain death or serious injury for the ultimate aphrodisiac of high-speed competition. Driving cars capable of over 200 miles per hour, they faced danger protected only by flimsy leather or fiberglass helmets, a set of light coveralls or a polo shirt, and an optional seat belt. (At the time, many European drivers still maintained that being tossed clear of a crashing car offered a better chance for survival.)

The dirt tracks and paved ovals where most professional competition took place were killing grounds for hundreds of drivers. Of the 33 men who started the 1955 "500," 18 would ultimately die at the wheel of a race car, including seven of the top ten finishers and all of the first five, including the brilliant, young winner, Bob Sweikert. Two more of the participants would suffer critical, career-ending injuries.

Sports car racing was somewhat safer, thanks to lower speeds and the use of wide, flat airport courses. Natural road circuits like Pebble Beach remained lethal, though, due to their tree-lined borders and drop-offs. During the main event of the sports car races at Pebble on March 22, 1956, popular ex-hot rodder Ernie McAfee was driving Los Angeles sportsman Bill Doheny's Ferrari 121LM when he missed a downshift entering a tight corner and slammed a stout Pine tree sideways. He was killed instantly, bringing the reality of carnage to the generally gentile world of sports car racing. His death would end the white tablecloth parties in the paddock hosted by San Francisco's Trader Vic's restaurant and cancel further racing on the Monterey Peninsula. The construction of the challenging Laguna

Seca road course farther inland was a reaction to the carnage as well.

After the horrific 1955 season, modest safety regulations were imposed in the form of roll bars, fireproof clothing, and improved crash helmets, but the danger levels remained gruesomely high compared to the relative safety enjoyed by today's drivers. Unintentionally counteracting the attempts to improve safety were the designers who steadily increased the performance of the race cars. Lightweight space frames, disc brakes, fuel injection, better tires, fiberglass bodies, and magnesium components were created lighter and faster automobiles. Experimentation with mid-engine designs was about to open a whole new door of technology that would revolutionize the sport by the end of the decade.

The Eliminator was totally obsolete. Not a single component was less than twenty years old and some could be dated to the middle 1920s. Most of the early hot rod-sports cars were by then hidden away in garages, never to see competition again until the vintage-racing craze arrived thirty years later. Only Livingstone and Max Balchowsky remained on the sports car scene with real hot rods.

Balchowsky was one of the towering characters in southern California motorsports. A hot-rodder to the core, he, like Livingstone, developed an interest in road racing in the early 1950s. Throughout the decade, Balchowsky created havoc among the purists with his pair of rumpled, Buick-powered specials called Ol' Yellers. These cars—in particular Ol' Yeller II—were insanely fast and regularly beat the best Ferraris fielded by Edgar and others.

As if to rub salt into the wounds of the purists, Balchowsky and his wife, Ina, campaigned their Ol' Yellers with white-wall tires, giving the tatty, canary yellow machines a semi-demented presence among the perfectly tailored Italian thoroughbreds. Even so, the future of sports car racing was clear: nowhere on the distant horizon did there seem any room for antediluvian devices like Ol' Yeller or the Eliminator. That speculation would turn out to be wrong, both in near and long term.

CHAPTER EIGHT
ELIMINATOR:
BEGINNING OF THE END

By 1958, the Go-Kart company was booming, thanks in part to sales based on the racetrack successes led by Livingstone. While he continued to race the Eliminator in Cal-Club road races and in occasional hill climbs at Tarzana, Arrowhead Springs, and Willow Springs, where he set quick times and was among the high finishers, he began to concentrate on karting competition and his ever-expanding business.

Within two years, scores of manufacturers were in on the act, building karts from coast to coast. Chainsaw and lawn-mower engines supplied by West Bend, Clinton, Tecumseh, and McCulloch were now specially tuned for karting. Two- and four-cycle powerplants, both in single- and twin-engine setups, were capable of touching 100 miles per hour with daredevil drivers.

By 1959, *Rod and Custom*, which had taken a primary role with editor Spencer Murray, a committed kart racer, listed 24 manufacturers on both the East and West Coasts. The pioneering Go-Kart company was in a leadership position, but there was much competition. Caretta, Dart-Kart, Bug, Lil 500, Mantis, Cad Cart, and Putt-Nick were but a sampling of the entrants into the steamy new market.

With the kart builders came a rush of accessory manufacturers offering special clutches, pistons, carburetors, exhaust manifolds, brakes, lubricants, and wheels and tires, which now included high-performance asphalt slicks.

Little did these eager entrepreneurs realize that they were on the threshold of a racing class that would, by the end of the century, be a training ground for scores of champions, ranging from NASCAR's Jeff Gordon to Ferrari superstar Michael Schumacher. By then, shifter karts and twin-engine lay-down versions would be capable of running at or near record speeds on most road courses and even on a few super speedways.

Within this pioneering world, Duffy Livingstone displayed amazing poise and skill on the racetrack. His years spent manhandling the cranky Eliminator had given him an advantage over his novice rivals. On his home track at Azuza and in races all over southern California and Mexico, Livingstone was a master of control aboard one of his tiny racers. In later years, the International Karting Federation would create a "Duffy Award" in recognition of his contribution to the sport.

The thriving Go-Kart business did not totally end Livingstone's racing with the Eliminator. The disastrous experiment with a torsion-bar rear suspension ended with a return to a single, rear leaf spring. A 1940 Ford unit mounted 17 inches behind the Halibrand quick-change rear end radically improved the handling. At the same time, Halibrand-knock-off magnesium wheels were installed in the back and a bracket for a Bell & Howell-surplus Air Force 16-millimeter gun camera was welded to the roll bar. The most important modification came in the form of a new Corvette Borg-Warner T-10 four-speed gearbox that Livingstone purchased from a local Chevrolet dealer. It replaced the old Cadillac-LaSalle three-speed that had done yeoman service and offered added flexibility in gear selection on the generally slow corners that dotted most of the road courses in the area.

Because he and his crew, consisting of his father Duke, brother Arnie, "Mooch" Vendevere, and Roy Desbrow, could easily remove the 1925 T-bucket's fenders, the Eliminator often raced both as a C-modified sports car (complete with headlights and trunk-mounted spare tire) or in "Formula Libre," a "run what you brung" class for open-wheel machinery of all kinds. His normal rivals in the latter contests were Terry Woods in a 1950 4.5-liter Talbot-Lago Grand Prix car and a flock of motorcycle-engined 500-cc Coopers and Keifts.

On one memorable afternoon at Paramount Ranch, Livingstone won the Formula Libre race and then, after starting at the back, nearly won the so-called "feature event" for the sports cars until sidelined with a mechanical failure.

As the 1958 racing season ended in the United States, there was irresistible pressure on both coasts for professional sports car racing. The simon-pure amateurism practiced by the SCCA, originally modeled on British prewar practices, was now being widely abused. Top drivers were defecting to Europe or other forms of the sport where the hypocrisy was less rampant. The "RFM" (Race for Money) movement gained strength by the day. Teams like Lance Reventlow's Scarab operations, John Edgar's Ferraris, and Briggs Cunningham's fleet of D-Type Jaguars operated at the highest level professionalism, yet they still raced for pewter mugs and silver trophies. This bordered on the absurd. Hardcore professionals like Carroll Shelby and Chuck Daigh hardly raced as a hobby, while other young guns, including Phil Hill, Dan Gurney, and Masten Gregory headed toward the Continent where at least a modest living could be made driving race cars.

Several futile attempts had been made to professionalize sports car racing as early as 1951. A small California Club, the Road Racing Register, ran a race for money at Willow Springs in 1956 and was supported by Tony Parravano, who enlisted Indianapolis stars Pat O'Connor and Jimmy Bryan to drive his Maseratis. Bryan won and Parravanno was banned by the SCCA for a year due to his sedition.

After the race, brush-cut, cigar-smoking Bryan, who was one of the greatest dirt track drivers of his day and would win Indianapolis in 1958, articulated the philosophical rift between oval track and road racing drivers: "Road racing is fun," he said after the race. "But the variation in speed bothers me. Fast and slow corners. I like to run like 'Jack the Bear' all the time." Ironically it would be his love of speed that would kill him on the ultrafast dirt circle at Langhorne, Pennsylvania, in 1960.

In May 1958, the United States Auto Club, which, after the tragic 1955 season, had taken over sanctioning of professional championship racing in the nation for the American Automobile Association, formed a road racing division. Its participants would race for filthy lucre, which outraged the purists in the SCCA even after such club stalwarts as Luigi Chinetti—the eastern importer for Ferrari—and John Fitch—driver for the Cunningham team and a Mercedes-Benz team member—were among the defectors.

A month earlier, the SCCA had reaffirmed its position, stating that any member taking money to race would be expelled. That policy turned to farce on October 12, 1958, when 70,000 spectators appeared at the new Riverside road course to witness a professional event co-sanctioned by the Cal-Club and USAC. The fans were treated to a sensational duel between Phil Hill in one of Edgar's potent 412 Ferraris and the winner Chuck Daigh in a Reventlow Scarab. Pandora's box opened.

In the meantime, Livingstone labored day and night with his Go-Kart business and the bubbling activity at his Kart track. The few races he ran with the Eliminator—now carrying a permanent number 184 and entered as the "Eliminator *Tihsepa* MK II" (until an SCCA official translated the dyslexic joke and banned the name)—were casual club affairs.

On occasion, the fun turned ugly. During a race at Santa Barbara's airport course, Livingstone tangled with the

Ferrari of Johnny von Neumann as they wrestled for the same bit of macadam in a tight corner. Both cars were dented but carried on to the finish. An angry von Neumann and several of his crewmen confronted Livingstone in the postrace paddock as he hammered away on the driver's door of his car. "What the hell are you whining about?" mused Livingstone. "It's easy to fix an aluminum Ferrari fender. But look at my door. It's dented real bad. You know how hard it is too find a Model-T door?" Von Neumann and crew stalked away, realizing they could not make headway with the unrepentant hot rodder.

Nineteen fifty-nine brought a tidal wave of professionals to sports car racing. Another major event at Pomona on March 8, 1959, was sanctioned by the USAC and the Cal Club, and was also sponsored by the *Los Angeles Examiner*— a rival of the *Times Mirror* that had backed the successful Riverside race six months earlier.

The race was to be held on the tight, two-mile course at the Los Angeles County Fairgrounds—later to be the scene of the enormously successful National Hot Rod Association's Winternationals drag races. Not only would USAC, the Cal-Club, and the *Examiner* team up for the event, but J. C. Agajanian, the well-known California oval track promoter and Indianapolis car owner who had won the "500" with a car driven by Troy Ruttman, aided in the promotion.

A tremendous roster of excellent drivers was among the 57-car entry. Top pro sports car drivers like Dan Gurney, Carroll Shelby, Ken Miles, Max Balchowsky (in Ol' Yeller II), and Chuck Daigh were to face off against USAC pros, including Jerry Unser (the older brother of Bobby and Al who was to die in a crash during practice at the Speedway two months later), Lloyd Ruby, Jim Rathmann, Tony Bettenhausen, and George Amick, who qualified 9th in Chuck Porter's Chevy-powered Mercedes-Benz 300SL. (Amick was also doomed to die within weeks at Daytona— amplifying the danger of racing in those days.) The roster also included top European Grand Prix drivers Wolfgang Von Trips, Ron Flockhart, Maurice Trintignant, and Roy Salvadori.

Sadly, Von Trips and the other Europeans would not have the opportunity to show their hands, having been hired by the promoters to come west on their way to the Sebring 12-Hours where they were to drive Ferraris and Aston Martins for money. At Pomona, they ended up in outclassed local machinery and were never factors in the race.

Duffy entered the Eliminator "on a lark," figuring at the very least he would be given, like all the entrants, 50 free gallons of racing gasoline and 20 quarts of oil. A quick trip to a photo lab created enough counterfeit pit passes to allow plenty of his friends to watch the fun. The event also attracted a crowd of 40,000 for the big race.

The sight of the ancient T-bucket parked in the paddock created the usual sneers from a crowd that included movie stars like Peter Ustinov, David Niven, Clark Gable, and honorary race queen Jayne Mansfield.

"What's that piece of junk doing here," asked a well-dressed Hollywood type as she gazed at the rumpled

Eliminator. "They felt sorry for the guy and let him enter it," replied her escort.

Duffy did not need a great deal of sympathy. In qualifying for the 75-lap 150-miler, he was 19th. That put him four seconds off Gurney's pole-winning time but on the grid ahead of such luminaries as Skip Hudson; Jim Rathmann, a future Indianapolis-500 winner; local star Bob Drake; Trintignant; Chaparral creator Jim Hall; Von Trips; former AAA National Driving Champion Tony Bettenhausen; and rising star Bruce Kessler. There was no widespread expression of sympathy for the aged machine among the competitors.

The race was a barn-burner among the fastest cars. These included Jerry Unser in Mickey Thompson's highly-modified Cadillac-powered Kurtis, Gurney in Frank Arciero's ex-Parravano 4.9 Ferrari, Carroll Shelby in John Edgar's 5.7 Maserati, Balchowsky's Ol' Yeller II, and the ultimate winner, Ken Miles in a Porsche 550 Spyder entered by local dealers Otto Zipper and Bob Estes (who as a kid had embarrassed Gable with his Model-T hot rod during a Santa Monica street race).

Livingstone drove well, shoving the aged Eliminator as high as eighth in the early stages, then making a long mid-race pit stop with cooling problems. Repairs were helped by a red-flag period that stopped the race after Bruce Kessler spun his powerful, Canadian-built Sadler MK I into a mass of parked cars near the starter's stand and badly injured himself and four spectators. This was the second such incident involving bystanders. On the first day of practice Sammy Weiss, driving an RSK Porsche, looped off the track and into a pack of flagmen, hurting several. In those days, crowd control had yet to develop beyond barriers of light fencing and a few hay bales, and such crashes were not uncommon.

Once the cooling problem had been cured, Livingstone returned to the battle well out of the hunt. Still, he pressed on, at one point passing young Skip Hudson, at the time considered the rising star in the sport, who was driving a well-prepared 300S Maserati. Being humbled by an ancient hot rod while at the wheel of a powerful, expensive, hand-built Italian sports car was not to be expected, especially among the purists lining the fence.

After the race, Hudson laughed about the incident with Livingstone. "I thought about pulling off the track and faking mechanical problems just so people wouldn't think I was that outclassed," he admitted.

Duffy ultimately finished 11th and fifth in the over 2-liter class in one of the strongest sports car fields ever assembled in the world up to that point. He took home $600 for his efforts. But the old car, even with its new T-10 four-speed transmission and hot Chevy engine, was hopelessly outdated. The monocoque Cooper-Monacos, lightweight Listers, and nimble Porsche RSs, RSKs, and RS60s were years ahead in terms of chassis, suspension, brakes, and aerodynamics. More advances would soon lead to the mid-engine revolution of the early 1960s.

He now added his increasingly famous Go-Kart logo to the hood of the Eliminator and continued to run in Cal

Club and SCCA races on an intermittent basis for the rest of the year. Meanwhile, his kart racing activities reached a fevered pitch.

It was clear that the fabled old machine that had confused, delighted, intrigued, and outraged so many people up and down the California coast was ready for retirement and a date with a junkyard crusher unless, of course, an odd confluence of events conspired to save it.

CHAPTER NINE
THE END OF THE BEGINNING

By 1960, Go-Kart manufacturing was on a roll. Karts and Mini-Bikes poured out of the Azuza factory by the thousands, while stacks of West Bend engines and miles of chrome-moly tubing waited to be transformed into product. The name was becoming generic to the sport, and promotion expanded into the big leagues. In 1959, Roy Desbrow had arranged a sponsorship deal with Indianapolis car owner and prosperous Arcadia body-shop operator "Ollie" Prather to carry the Go-Kart logo on his two-year-old Kurtis-Kraft 500G roadster at Indianapolis. Assigned to drive it was journeyman driver Bill Homier, a 41-year-old midget ace and Warner Brothers employee who had entered the "500" for six years but had qualified only once 1954—an effort that ended with a wall-whacking after 33 laps.

While Livingstone remained in California, Desbrow and Rowles had gone east to Indianapolis where the Prather car burned a piston in practice and never qualified. But heady with their exposure to the big leagues, they had returned to Azuza with high hopes for 1960.

With another sponsorship set with Prather, a clever American Indian whose fortune was sourced from a Government settlement with his tribe years earlier, the Go-Kart company returned to Indianapolis in May 1960, with Homier again the assigned driver.

Though having spent $8,000 to sponsor the Prather car, the Go-Kart company's chances for success at the Brickyard were limited at best. This time Livingstone went east to protect his investment. He found the garage area, known as "Gasoline Alley," packed with Offenhauser/Meyer-Drake powered roadsters owned for the most part by dilettantes and wrenched by copycat mechanics. "One guy would change his exhaust system or the air intake and half the other guys would copy him," Livingstone recalled. "They were all stuck in a rut except for a few bright guys who took chances."

Virtually every car in the garage area had been built either by Kurtis-Kraft, A. J. Watson, Eddie Kuzma, Quinn Epperly, or were one-off variations thereof. All were offset roadster chassis riding on Firestone tires and Monroe shock absorbers with Halibrand disc brakes, two-speed gearboxes, and rear ends. The engines were 4.2-liter, four-cylinder, DOHC Meyer-Drake/Offenhausers equipped with Champion spark plugs, Hillborn fuel injection, Joe Hunt Magnetos, Carillo connecting rods, and Sparks True-Forge pistons. Except for the eastern-built tires, plugs, and shocks, all such equipment could trace its origins to the southern California hot-rod and racecar cultures.

Go-Kart was not the only karting manufacturer represented in big-time automobile racing. The same year, none other than A. J. Foyt was campaigning a sprint car in United States Auto Club competition sponsored by Dart-Kart and built by Mickey Rupp of Mansfield, Ohio, himself a part-time race driver. "Dart-Kart" had been one of the names originally suggested by Lynn Wineland back in 1956 when "Go-Kart" had been selected. It would be Rupp's firm, albeit a late arrival in the market, that would outlast its earlier, original inspiration in the field.

Livingstone quickly noted that pit stop changes of the big Firestone tires (essentially based on commercial truck designs) involved hammering away at a three-prong knockoff wing-nut mounting a Halibrand magnesium wheel on a six-pin hub, then banging the nut back in place. At the time, the cars were using nitrogen-powered air-jacks and Livingstone suggested to Prather that the same energy source be employed with an air-wrench on a single, large lug-nut. That would save valuable seconds in the pits. The idea was rejected, based on the conventional wisdom that no one else had tried it. Years would pass before such a wheel-changing system would come into widespread use at Indianapolis.

The Go-Kart effort at the vaunted "500" was a disaster. Homier never got the car up to speed and failed to make a qualifying attempt. He was replaced by Eddie Russo, whose uncle, Paul, was one of the top drivers at the time and whose father, Joe, had been killed in 1934 in Langhorne,

Pennsylvania. Russo managed to make the starting field in the 29th spot.

Like Homier, he had tried to qualify for the big race since 1954 with dismal results, capped in 1957 when he was bunted on the backstretch during a pace lap and never took the green flag.

On race morning, the Go-Kart Kurtis-Kraft 500G (now three years old) was rolled onto the grid, but its driver was nowhere in sight. As the countdown to the start continued and "Back Home in Indiana" was being trilled by movie star Dennis Morgan, Russo finally rushed up to the car. He had loaned his pit pass to a friend and was not allowed into the garage area for a few tense moments before the guards were finally convinced he was a driver.

He should have stayed home. Russo lazed in the ruck as Rodger Ward and Jim Rathmann carried on a furious duel for the lead. Russo finally lost it in the second turn, bashed into the concrete wall, and ended up being hauled off to Methodist Hospital. His career ended there with a concussion and ruptures of the spleen and kidneys.

In yet another strange coincidence for Livingstone, who was handling left rear tire changes in the Prather pits, Russo's crash happened on lap 84.

Homier, in the meantime, had found another ride for the race in a Kuzma chassis and started 31st behind Russo. He held on, drove steadily and finished 13th, his last and best effort in the "500."

The Prather-Russo debacle at the Speedway in May 1960 may have symbolically served as a high-water mark for the

Go-Kart Manufacturing Company, at least in terms of national exposure. While the name had gained universal identity, the firm itself was facing every-increasing competition. Like the early days of the automobile industry in the first decade of the twentieth century, hundreds of upstart operations tried to get into the karting act. After all, manufacturing only required a batch of tubing, wheels, lawn-mower engines, and a welder to enter the business.

As Livingstone raised the bar in competition with a variety of powerful engine combinations and therefore kept Go-Kart in the headlines, warfare on the business front increased exponentially. Better organized and larger firms entered the field with sophisticated distribution and manufacturing capabilities. Prices dropped, based on the eternal laws of supply and demand.

Go-Kart quality stayed high, but its name had been diluted to a point where virtually every rival machine in the field was carrying the name in sub-rosa fashion. With three muffler shops, Debrow, a man ill-trained in business practices beyond simple book-keeping, was overwhelmed by the complexities of the expanding kart market. Livingstone, in the meantime, was concentrating on low-volume manufacturing and racing while Rowles, a former surplus scrap dealer, could offer little in the way of sophisticated business planning.

It became clear, first to Desbrow, that the little firm could not survive in the increasingly competitive marketplace. In late 1962, he cashed out of the business, leaving Livingstone and Rowles to swim upstream alone.

Livingstone slowly lost interest in the Eliminator, briefly buying an OSCA 1600 sports racing car from an East-Coast owner, Bill Lloyd, for $2,600. The little machine, once raced by Stirling Moss, would remain in his possession briefly before he resold it for a small profit, only to learn years later that it had passed through a European auction for over $500,000.

As the demands of the Go-Kart Company increased, the Eliminator was only sporadically raced, finally ending its original career at a 1960 Cal-Club event at Pomona, when the Chevy engine's tired crankshaft broke. Livingstone hauled the old car back to his Monrovia shop, yanked out the damaged block, and placed it under a workbench. The car, battered and ignored, was doomed to the back of the shop where it would sit in isolation for over ten years.

Livingstone would later salvage the engine and gearbox for use in a 1927 Ford roadster, utilizing a radiator shell molded from the original Emil Diedt design.

Now married to first wife Gloria, Duff was in the process of raising two children: son Terry, now owner of a successful contracting business, and daughter Kim, who would grow up to become the director of Primates at the famed San Diego Zoo. Livingstone and Rowles steadily lost ground in the increasingly competitive karting business, which had now expanded to both Europe and South America.

The end came in 1963 when the Go-Kart Manufacturing Company declared bankruptcy and Livingstone returned to the muffler business in Monrovia. He settled back into a trade that permitted him time to race karts, winning three

Duffy with car at Pete Chapouris' shop during restoration. *Pat Ganahl*

Duffy in car with Pete Chapouris (center) and Pete Eastwood (right). *Pat Ganahl*

The cockpit of the Eliminator prior to restoration. *Pat Ganahl*

The Eliminator was torn down to its bare chassis during restoration.

Pete Eastwood tests the bare chassis of the Eliminator in front of Pete Chapouris'
Pomona shop during the summer of 1997.

Duffy checks out the Eliminator cockpit 40 years later. *Pat Ganahl*

The Eliminator in racing form (note the larger roll bar) at Watkins Glen, 1997.
Bert Skidmore drove the car to third place. *Gordon Jolley*

Watkins Glen, 1997. Note the flat handling. *Gordon Jolley*

Does a hot rod handle? Monterey, 2000. Note the attitude of the D-type Jaguar that Skidmore has just passed.

Barry Brown dyno-tests at Kennedy Automotive in Niagara Falls, New York.

At the Grand Island, New York Road Race 50th Anniversary re-creation, July 2002.

Fun with the old car at Grand Island, New York. Yates with his son-in-law, Robert Lilly, riding shotgun. *Steve Rossini*

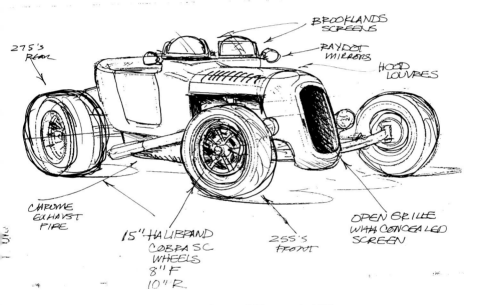

SUGGESTIONS
TO TOM
TAYLOR

BROOKLANDS
SCREENS

RAYDOT
MIRRORS

HOOD
LOUVRES

275's
REAR

CHROME
EXHAUST
PIPE

15" HALIBRAND
COBRA SC
WHEELS
8" F
10" R

255's
FRONT

OPEN GRILLE
WITH CONCEALED
SCREEN

Preliminary drawing of the new Eliminator by Brock Yates, early 1998.

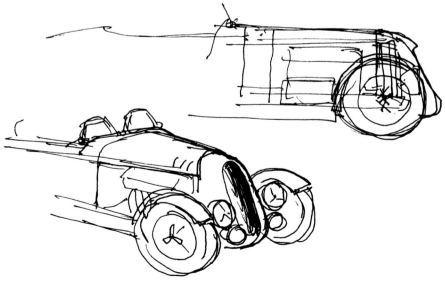

RADIATOR
FUELCELL
TRUCK CYLINDER HEADS
SEATS
WILWOOD RACING BRAKES
FASTENERS —
HOSES —

Preliminary drawing of the new Eliminator by Brock Yates, early 1998.

The Viper engine is longer, but only 60 pounds heavier than the Chevrolet small-block V-8.

The New Eliminator. *Neil Rashba*

National championships and a seat on the International Karting Federation Board of Directors that he was to hold for 21 years.

In December 1973, a young Laverne, California, enthusiast named Buzz Shoemaker spotted the Eliminator at Livingstone's Monrovia shop. He inquired if the car was for sale and quickly struck a deal. Duffy sold him the car, minus engine, transmission, and the front axle, for $100.

Fearing that the old car would scratch his new Ford pickup, Shoemaker lined the bed with cardboard before loading up the aged wreck.

Planning to restore the car, the Eliminator's new owner replaced the front axle with an exact duplicate and slowly searched out bits that would permit it to be added to his growing collection of vintage sprint cars. After a few years, other interests distracted Shoemaker, and the Eliminator was sold once again—this time to brilliant cigar-chomping race-car fabricator, restorer, and sometime race driver Chuck Porter.

Charles Earl Porter was one of the great characters on the southern California automotive scene. Like most of his contemporaries, he was a World War II veteran, having won the "Distinguished Flying Cross" for a truly phenomenal feat as a waist gunner in a B-17. After flying nearly 60 missions over Germany, his plane, named "Old Bill," was ravaged by antiaircraft fire. The entire crew, save for Porter and the radio operator, was killed. Somehow the pair, untrained to fly, managed to improvise their way back to England though where they crash-landed the bomber and survived. Later, flying over Japan, Porter's B-29 was shot down over Nagasaki. He bailed out, was imprisoned, and survived the subsequent atomic bomb that exploded only nine miles from his cell six months later.

Porter's shops on the corner of Sunset and Vermont in Hollywood opened in 1950, and he became known as one of the finest metal-men in the nation. His work graced all manner of exotic cars owned by the likes of Lance Reventlow, James Dean, and Steve McQueen.

Again, the car was relegated to the back of a busy shop, where a number of witnesses recall seeing it sitting in a dark corner, ignored and presumably awaiting restoration.

The next owner was Gordon Hall, a former Hughes Tool Company machinist who had retired to a small ranch on the northwestern edge of Tucson, Arizona. A dabbler in old sports cars and a member of the Porsche Club of America, Hall told friends he had purchased the car from Porter and planned a restoration. But his cactus-dotted yard was littered with wrecked and abandoned sports cars of all types, and how-and-when he intended to deal with the Eliminator remained unknown. Hall has now passed to his reward and cannot answer the one major mystery that lingers.

All those who saw the car at Hall's Tucson home and recorded its presence with numerous photographs recall a new element: someone had reinstalled a flathead Ford V-8 in the chassis and mounted sprint-car-style nerf bars ahead of the rear wheels, now mounted with Firestone dirt track racing tires.

The Ford was clearly set up for competition, with Weiand aluminum cylinder heads and a dual intake manifold with Stromberg 97 carburetors. But who installed it remains lost in time. Sadly Chuck Porter died in 1982, suffering a heart attack while running his Kurtis-Kraft Offy in a vintage-midget race and cannot aid in the investigation. Was it him? Or a customer? It appears that someone intended to restore the Eliminator for some form of vintage-roadster racing—hence the addition of nerf bars and the dirt track tires. Beyond that, the details of the conversion, which was cursory and incomplete at best, remain an enigma. Amazingly, through the long neglect and the sporadic efforts at restoration, Duffy Livingstone's original paint scheme, numbers and decals remained untouched, though someone had attempted to paint over the "Go-Kart" logos on the hood.

In 1987, Hall decided to sell the old hot rod, which thankfully he had not touched. He asked fellow PCA member Jeff Gamble to broker the car for him. Gamble, a well-known Tucson-based automotive sculptor, placed classified ads in the June 27 issue of *National Speed Sport News*. He had learned some history about the car from his neighbor, Jay Chamberlain—the now-retired Lotus driver and distributor who had helped start the whole Eliminator saga forty years earlier.

Gamble's ad read:

> For Sale: Vintage dirt track-T or run as a
> vintage sports car, documents from 1950s
> event with a 265 Chevy engine, Halibrand
> quickie, rear wheels, flat head and spares.
> $8,000 or best offer.

The price—over 80 times the value of the car 20 years before—was a reflection of the rising value of cars of all types that could be employed in the booming sport of vintage racing.

Hall had owned the Eliminator for better than eight years, during which time it had sat outside, ignored and neglected among his hulks and automotive rubble. Thankfully, the arid, low-humidity climate had served as a perfect location in which to preserve the old machine. Its tenure with Hall had done it little damage.

While Gamble's ad produced a small response, including one serious inquiry from a well-known Ohio race car restorer, it was a local friend and fellow Porsche Club member who ended up with the Eliminator. Tom Murphy, a prominent Tucson attorney and fellow member of the PCA chapter, had been toying with the idea of restoring a Porsche 356 for vintage racing. Through Gamble, he heard about the Hall hot rod and became intrigued.

As a great fan of the Monterey Historics and Pebble Beach Concours d'Elegance weekend, Murphy thought the old T-bucket could be sufficiently restored to compete at Laguna Seca. But based on the condition of the bodywork, participation on the patrician Pebble Beach fairways seemed out of the question. (Both famed affairs lay in the car's future.) On a whim, he forked over the necessary cash to Hall and beamed like a school boy as the ownership transfer was made in his driveway.

Murphy quickly called his old Loyola University roommate, Pat Ganahl, in Los Angeles. Ganahl was a fine automotive journalist and well-known hot-rod historian. "Hey, I bought a hot rod!" Murphy exclaimed—a serious confession from a hardcore Porschefile.

"Yeah, what's it all about?" asked Ganahl.

Murphy described the car; T-bucket body. Red and white paint. Number 184.

"Holy cats," yelled Ganahl. "Do you know what you've got? That's the Eliminator! One of the most famous of the California road racing hot rods. I haven't seen or heard of that thing in over ten years!"

Now what to do with the battered, old beast, regardless of its heritage? After sitting in Murphy's garage for eight months, he made arrangements with friend and fellow Porsche enthusiast Mike Springer to have it shipped to Springer's Custom Carrier Truck Lines garage in Fullerton, California. There, his director of maintenance, John Nevins, would undertake the restoration. An experienced craftsman and fabricator, Nevins had restored a pair of Porsche 356s for Springer and a Mini-Cooper S. He was well qualified to undertake restoration of the Eliminator along with his duties as the maintenance chief of his boss' fleet of trucks. Or so it seemed.

Nevins quickly realized he faced a major challenge in getting the Eliminator back to running condition. Tom Murphy wanted power from a small-block Chevy instead of the flathead Ford, desiring reliability and also seeking to restore the car to the configuration in which it enjoyed its greatest successes. Nevins sold the Ford and replaced it with a used Chevy V-8, bored out to 283 cubic inches. He linked it to a fresh four-speed T-10 transmission and set out to correctly replace the front suspension bits taken by Livingstone for his 1929 roadster.

Scouring automotive swap meets at Veteran's stadium and at the Pomona fairgrounds, Nevins found the pieces needed to fabricate new radius rods and front suspension linkages, in keeping with photos supplied by Duffy and from old magazine stories. At the time, Livingstone had opened a Costa Mesa welding shop called Super Weld, so sharing information had been easy. Duffy sold Murphy the original exhaust headers he had fabricated in 1956 for the Chevy and kept when the car had been sold. The price was $400, four times what he had charged for the entire car 16 years earlier.

Nevins worked hard to keep the Eliminator authentic, although per Murphy's instructions, he removed—but carefully preserved—Livingstone's original roll bar and replaced it with a larger unit for safety purposes. The rear suspension, which had been cobbled by someone with an attempt to use torsion bars, had to be tossed away and the original Duffy transverse leaf-spring version rebuilt. After finding a correct Halibrand center section and rear-axle assembly, Nevins' truck-maintenance work overwhelmed him. Complicating matters, Custom Carriers moved from Fullerton to nearby Anaheim. The Eliminator project ground to a halt.

Another seven years had passed following Murphy's purchase. His interest waned as any chance of completing the project seemed light years in the future. He called Pat Ganahl and asked him to sell the Eliminator. Its price, based on escalating values in the vintage-car market, would be over three times what he had paid Gordon Hall in 1988.

I spotted Ganahl's ad in the November 1996 issue of *Hemmings Motor News*, the car collector's monthly bible. Seeing the word "Eliminator" flashed me back to 1956 and Montgomery Field. There it was, that cranky, old hot-rod juking around the course, totally and completely out of place—Jed Clampett at the Opera—outraging and infuriating the *tifosi*. I was overcome with an insatiable desire to possess that wonderful old machine.

A quick call to Ganahl. Some brief haggling over the price. Pat wanted the 18-inch rear Halibrands. I consented.

A price was reached. Tom Murphy said we had a deal, a bank draft was overnighted.

I owned the Eliminator. A car I had not laid eyes on in forty-one years and would not see again for eight more months.

I knew the story was just beginning.

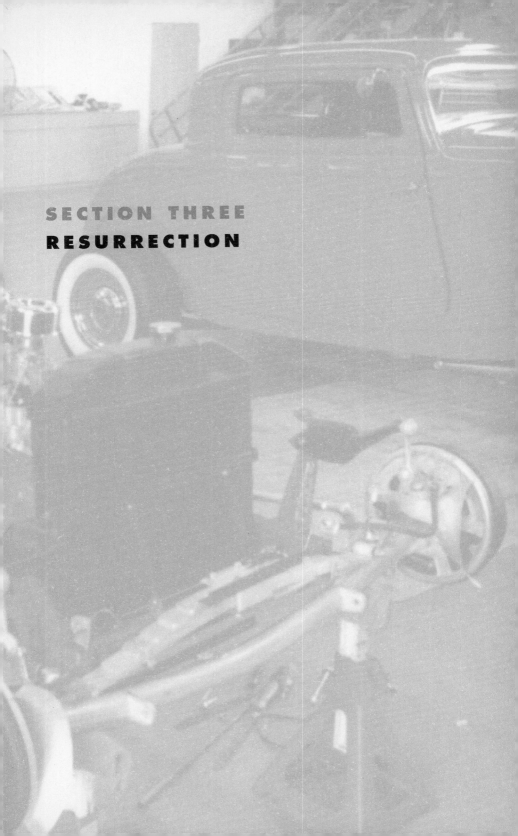

SECTION THREE
RESURRECTION

CHAPTER TEN
THE REVIVAL BEGINS

I had known Kirk White since the early 1970s. He supplied the Ferrari 275GTB that Dan Gurney and I drove to a record-breaking cross-country victory in the 1972 Cannonball Sea-to-Shining Sea Memorial Trophy Dash. Several years later, I purchased a Ferrari 250GT/L Lusso coupe from Kirk's Philadelphia exotic car dealership, and we had remained friends long after he had moved to New Smyrna Beach, Florida. There he began dealing in collectible gas-powered model cars of the type that young Duffy Livingstone had raced at the Rose Bowl in the late 1930s.

Kirk was also brokering original hot rods and had become an expert in the field, owning several of the most unique and original machines from the glory days of the late 1940s and early 1950s. We had shared information about my purchase of the Eliminator, and he was my first choice to consult about where the car ought to be restored.

"Pete Chapouris is your man," said White during a telephone call made only days after my purchase.

Of course. Chapouris was a powerhouse in the hot rod industry. He was the original "Pete" in the well-known "Pete and Jake's" hot rod supply business and now ran his own restoration shop, PC3G, in Pomona, California.

Chapouris' towering reputation in the business both as a hardcore street rodder and as a craftsman was unparalleled. Cars from his shop had won major prizes at prestigious events, such as the Oakland Roadster show. His facility on Grand Avenue in Pomona, east of Los Angeles, was near Pasadena where, coincidently, the Eliminator had been built nearly fifty years earlier. It was surgically clean and laden with state-of-the art equipment for vehicle restoration with a specific concentration on hot rods.

As a kid, Chapouris had been employed at Don Blair's Speed Shop, the famous Pasadena hot rod landmark situated across the street from where the Eliminator had been fabricated in the 1950s. His cars had starred in movies, including Martin Sheen's *California Kid,* and he had built a veritable fleet of highly visible, much-publicized rods and custom motorcycles for ZZ Top superstar Billy F. Gibbons. He has been inducted into the *Hot Rod* magazine's Hall of Fame and named as one of the top 100 most influential people in the high-performance industry. In a word, his credentials were impeccable.

Having never met Chapouris but being familiar with his work and reputation, I took Kirk's advice and called him. He was direct and businesslike, yet an affable conversationalist. I immediately liked and trusted him, finding he embodied many of the characteristics found in men involved in the American motorsport industry. They are generally devoid of arrogance or artifice, the epitome of Yankee honesty and candor. The demands of motorsports—perhaps best described by that aged canard, "the bullshit stops when the green flag drops"—permit only the genuine article to survive. Fakers and phonies simply disintegrate in a world where only results count.

I knew Pete Chaprouis and I could do business. Pat Ganahl had sent snapshots of the Eliminator parked in its Fullerton warren; a rental storage room filled with the car and a few boxes of parts, most of which would disappear. What was saved was the original Livingstone roll bar, exhaust pipes, and the basic chassis and drivetrain.

After trailering the car back to his shop, Chapouris reported that much work needed to be done, especially in the rear suspension, which was incomplete and historically inaccurate. After accessing photos from various publications and speaking with Duffy Livingstone, who was now living in Grants Pass, Oregon, with his second wife, Dee Dee, Chapouris told me that Pete Eastwood, his friend and top-flight fabricator, would be assigned to restore it. This would entail complete disassembly, sandblasting the frame, rebuilding the suspension, and fresh paint.

But the question of the rumpled old body remained. Some advised that it should be totally restored and returned to its original, pristine state with fresh paint, numbers, and decals. Others maintained it should be kept the way it was found.

"You can't restore 'original,'" my wife Pamela commented.

"What do you want to do about the body?" asked Chapouris during one of dozens of coast-to-coast conversations about the restoration.

"Let's keep it the way it is," I said. "Original is original, dents and all."

"Thank God," said Pete. "I was worried that you'd want brand new. That would have ruined one of the truly rare pieces of American hot rod art."

One major challenge with the body had to be overcome. At some point in the distant past, prior to the car's arrival at Gordon Hall's Tucson home, the "Go-Kart" logo had been painted over with a light coat of white primer, perhaps as an initial attempt to restore the entire body. Now this coating would have to be removed by using special solvent that would not damage the original logo. So, too, would the small "Go-Kart" decal on the nose be preserved as well as the original numbers and decals if possible. Of particular interest was a crude "C" formed out of electrical tape on the left side of the body. Placed there in 1959 by Livingstone, it was a designation that the Eliminator was running in "C-Modified," a class for cars carrying engines over 1500-cc (91 cubic inches). Somehow, the tape had remained in place for over thirty years—a testimony to the unknown brand of tape's incredible adhesive qualities—and had to be saved.

Thanks to Chapouris' staff of craftsman, all of these goals were met.

The project went forward with me still never having seen the car and placing total faith in a man I had never met, separated by 3,000 miles.

A series of photographs and a constant stream of bills (Chapouris had been in the business too long to work on speculation) would arrive from Pomona to keep me updated on the progress.

Duffy and his old pal, famed *Hot Rod* magazine cartoonist Tom Medley, visited the shop. The word was out among the southern California hot rod community about the project. A stream of the sport's Brahmins, including Wally Parks, now a vibrant and active 86 years old, arrived to view Eastwood's impeccable work.

Also appearing was hot rod icon Alex Xydias, whose pioneering So-Cal streamliners had set repeated records on the dry lakes, often driven by future *Road & Track* editor and historian, the late Dean Batchelor. Before moving into magazine work, Batchelor had driven one of Xydias' So-Cal Specials at a record-shattering 193 miles per hour at Bonneville. But Xydias' visit to examine the Eliminator had other purposes. At the time, he and Chapouris were in negotiations to revive the So-Cal Speed Shop name—one of the most recognizable in the business. This would happen in 1998, with PG3G becoming the So-Cal Speed Shop with several franchised outlets around the nation.

Sadly, the front brake ducts Livingstone had fabricated from a Japanese army helmet he had brought home from the South Pacific had long gone missing. Eastwood scoured area military-surplus and memorabilia stores in search of a replacement. Unable to find an exact original, he settled for a Bolivian army helmet, which had been copied from the Japanese version in perfect dimensions. Such compromises are sometimes necessary in restoration projects.

Also missing were the Halibrand wheels that Duffy had used in various sizes and dimensions. The original, solid magnesium versions dating to the early 1950s were difficult to find, but Eastwood succeeded, finding a set of four, then having them magnafluxed and totally renovated.

The small-block Chevy engine was replaced by a fresh unit from Barry Gowen, a long-time engine builder who also ran the Summit Racing shop in Talmage, Ohio. Having worked with the Summit people in the past, I employed Gowen's expertise to create a new engine rather than taking any risks with the Los Angeles counterpart found with the car. Chapouris did not do engine rebuilding and felt comfortable with the Summit option. The new powerplant was finished in May 1997, complete with a vintage Edelbrock intake manifold mounting three Stromberg 97 carburetors. The aluminum Borg-Warner T-10 transmission was in good shape and, after an examination, was deemed good to go in the car. A shift linkage fabrication was similar to the stock General Motors unit, which made Livingstone immensely proud that he had designed it before seeing a contemporary factory linkage.

The rear suspension offered the most challenge. Nevins had done good work up to the point where the project stopped at Custom Carriers. But Eastwood found that the spring he had planned to employ was too short and the shackles were too long. "We've got to find a correct 41 Ford spring like Duff used," said Chapouris by phone. "This sort of accuracy in restoration is like having straight teeth," he said, making sense with his broad analogy. A proper 140 pound, 1941 Ford spring was located and the resulting rear suspension was exactly like Livingstone's.

Work proceeded through the spring and early summer of 1997 with a regular supply of photographs sent to me, offering encouraging proof that the restoration was being done to the highest standards.

Feeling optimistic about the progress, I entered the Monterey Historics set for the last week in August. As usual, there was a last-minute rush to complete the project. On August 15 I received a letter from Jerry Forster, the PC3G General Manager stating, "We had two to four guys working on the car full-time for the past two weeks. Mike Cardenas and Dennis McNeil actually slept at the shop several nights to make sure everything was accomplished on time. Not surprisingly, the hours devoted to the car over the last two weeks have been extensive. The only loose ends are the correct gauges, which Pete [Eastwood] will obtain.

"As a small gesture of appreciation, the transport and Pete Eastwood's time up at Monterey are on us. Thank you for the opportunity to restore this significant vehicle."

Clearly, the restoration of the Eliminator was being carried out by a first-class operation employing the highest standards. There are a number of superb restoration shops dotted around the nation, but Kirk White's recommendations to seek out Pete Chapouris and his enterprise—soon to be known as the So-Cal Speed Shop—proved to be key to the revival of the Eliminator. Now, as it headed to the race-tracks and on the show circuit, the rest would be up to me.

CHAPTER ELEVEN
BACK ON TRACK

While I had not met him personally I had known Barry Brown by reputation for a number of years. His Riter Restoration business in East Rochester, New York, had a fine reputation in the field of classic car renovation, and he was an obvious choice to maintain the Eliminator after it had amazed and outraged the throngs at the Monterey Historics in August 1997.

During a long lunch with Brown and mutual friend Sam Turner, a lifelong car nut and veteran vintage racer at my Cannonball Run Pub in Wyoming, New York, we reached an agreement whereby Riter Restoration would maintain the Eliminator for future races and shows. It was during this session that talk of a replica Eliminator first arose. I had long dreamed of building a car of my own, with design themes that melded early hot rods and sports-racing cars with a modern, drivetrain and running gear. The Eliminator seemed to be a perfect launch pad, and Turner, who was on the verge of retiring from a successful insurance business, offered his enthusiastic support if such a project was started.

The Eliminator was hauled across the country by Passport trucking and delivered to Barry's shop, a cluttered but efficient space in a small industrial park located near a major Amtrak freight route. Several changes had to be made before the Eliminator would be ready for more competition. Duffy Livingstone's original roll bar, its small hoop being a flimsy seatback from a late 1950s Go-Kart, had to be replaced. While original and representing Livingstone's welding skills, it afforded limited protection to the driver in the event of a rollover. Barry and his two master craftsman associates who were also his cousins, Jim and Bob Jeffords, removed the T-bucket body, carefully took out the old roll bar, and replaced it with a larger, stronger unit. The rubber brake lines installed by Eastwood, while authentic and probably safe, were replaced by modern, braided-steel versions.

It was also decided that the old, solid disc Halibrand wheels were too rare and valuable to risk on the racetrack in the future. They would be replaced by a set of replica bean-hole Halibrands to be ordered from P/S Wheels in Torrance, California.

A more substantial, modern bucket-seat was installed for the driver with full six-point belting. The old warrior was ready for battle.

There were no plans to campaign the car on a regular basis. Vintage racing in America has developed into an intense sport, with a regular cadre of teams who compete in a number of sanctioning bodies, including California's Historic Motorsports Association (HMSA), the Florida-based Historic Sports Racing (HSR), and the Sports Car Vintage Racing Association (SVRA)—the latter being the largest and most active on the East Coast.

The plan was to enter the Eliminator in the Zippo United States Vintage Grand Prix at Watkins Glen on the weekend of September 4–7, 1997. Having already determined that I would not fit in the car and assigning Barry—who was an accomplished amateur driver—to handle the mechanical chores, Bert Skidmore became an obvious candidate.

Arrangements were made for him to fly east to drive the Eliminator. An added incentive for the visit was that he was dating Kim Harmon, a comely young official of the SVRA.

The class of cars the Eliminator would be up against would be formidable. It included late 1950s machines with radically more advanced technology. Group Four in the SVRA was, at the time, dominated by two cars: Bob Fergus, a veteran sports car driver, in a perfectly-prepared Lotus 15 and John Harden, the Oklahoma City restoration expert who regularly drove sportsman Syd Silverman's powerful 1958 Lister Chevrolet "Knobbly." Fergus' Lotus, weighing barely half-a-ton yet powered by a lusty two-liter Coventry Climax four-cylinder producing over 200 horsepower, was a handling gem that could match the Lister's big power advantage even on a giant track like Watkins Glen. Also entered in the Zippo were Vic Edelbrock, Jr., scion of the famed high-performance opera-tion, in a sleek, Costin-bodied Lister Chevy; John Higgins in a lovely 1959 Porsche RSK; plus three other Listers, eight Lotuses, three powerful but ill-handling Cadillac-Allard J2X roadsters, and one very quick Elva Mk III with a 1.5-liter Coventry Climax driven by veteran Alex Quattlebaum.

If the Eliminator produced curious stares at Laguna Seca, it was viewed as an intruder from another planet at Watkins Glen. Hot rods on the East Coast are essentially unknown in sports car circles, and when the Eliminator was unloaded in the garage area, looks of open disdain spread among those who examined the car. Endless questions about how and why such a beast would dare to appear among the surrounding exotica reached the point of tedium. It was agreed among our little crew, which included Summit's Barry Gowen who had built the engine, that a sign explaining the car must be prepared for future events.

The curiosity turned to amazement during the third practice session. Though he had never seen the racetrack, Bert took to its sweeping corners and wooly downhill section easily. He began turning impressive times and, when the session ended, he felt increasingly comfortable with the car, though not surprisingly, he noted that the old machine's barn-door aerodynamics seriously impeded its speed on the Glen's long uphill straight.

As expected, Fergus set quick time ahead of Harden in the Lister, although John was given a small jab of reality when Skidmore passed him on the pit straightaway in a surprisingly potent burst of speed. Following the session Harden appeared, still in his driver's suit, to examine the old machine that he had earlier ignored. Others appeared as well to peer at the relic, understanding now that a renegade from California was on the prowl.

As it had done for all of its competitive life, the Eliminator was behaving badly, shaming proper thorough-breds on the track and horrifying the purists with its tatty presence in the pits.

Skidmore qualified fifth in a field of 23 cars, a tenth of a second slower than the Harden, but two seconds off Fergus' pace, and slower than Jonathan Evans' Lister-Chevy, Higgins RSK, and Cap Chenowith's Lola MK I, all by a small margin.

The race would be a six-lap sprint. Power and handling would be the key since no tire advantage was permitted. At Monterey, all cars were required to run older version, hard-compound Dunlop radials to level the playing field and prevent dangerous suspension and drivetrain overloading on the old machinery with modern, high-adhesion rubber.

Skidmore finished third. He was smooth and quick, never putting a wheel wrong. Harden won over Quattlebaum's Lotus. Race favorite Fergus retired, as did Evans, Higgins, and Chenworth, all factors that might have driven us deeper into the finishing field. We were delighted with Burt's so-called "podium" finish. For his effort, he was given a special Case jack-knife and a trophy—standard rewards in the world of simon-pure amateur competition.

The Eliminator had come east to once again shock and amaze. This was getting to be fun.

Hardly a pedigreed member of the elite, at least the car had credibility with the Antique Automobile Club of America. The club certified the Eliminator as a race car in its

Class 24-B in time for the Watkins Glen race. After examining the car's history and provenance based on extensive records and photographs the club had no doubts regarding the car's significance. For future generations, this certification would establish the heritage of an automobile that was rapidly heading toward its 50th birthday.

Races were hardly the sole diversion provided by the Eliminator. In March 1998 we decided to enter the car in the prestigious Amelia Island Concours d' Elegance, one of the finest car shows in the world that traditionally attracted world-class exotics of the same caliber that appeared at Pebble Beach and Meadowdale.

Run by Bill Warner, a long-time sports car racer, photographer, and journalist, the Amelia Island event was a perfect opener for the collector car season, set on the golf course adjacent to the five-star Ritz Carlton Hotel, which served as the event's headquarters for a black-tie banquet and the scene of a high-dollar car auction.

It was into this pristine world of perfectly-preened and polished automobiles and blue-blazer Brahmins that the dreaded machine would intrude, again to shock, outrage, and amuse.

I was selected to be one of a group of judges for the Concours, which left little or no time to polish up the old beast before it was to be examined by other judges. Pamela and I hauled the car south in our truck and trailer and unloaded it among a fleet of giant transporters packed with perfect Packards, Ferraris, Rolls-Royces, and the like. As always, the Eliminator was out of place.

While the day of the Concours dawned bright and sunny, a hard rain the night before had left the fairways of the golf course, where the grand collection of machinery would be displayed, soft and loamy. This demanded much care in moving the cars into position, lest the grass be riven with tire gouges and unseemly ruts.

Winning anything at an event such as Amelia Island is a highly coveted achievement for car collectors, many of whom spend their lives and substantial fortunes collecting, restoring, and displaying rare and exotic automobiles. Many of the cars that appear at such events are never driven other than the times they are eased out of their heated and air conditioned garages and into enclosed transporters for trips to and from the Concours. These machines are known in the hobby as "trailer queens," and, while they are kinetic sculpture of the first-rank, somehow they cease to be real automobiles and descend into the world of mechanical fetishism.

The extreme example that year was a Mercedes-Benz 300S convertible that my team judged and was awarded a blue ribbon. The owner was sufficiently anal about his possession and refused to even allow a judge—a man with a worldwide reputation in the field—to place the ribbon on his windshield. Touching of any kind in the presence of this presumed automotive royalty was apparently verboten.

This was hardly the case with the Eliminator, which attracted a large crowd, essentially out of curiosity. I had placed a small sign in the cockpit that read, "If you don't understand, don't bother asking." This relieved some of the puzzlement, but I had little hope of being selected for any kind of an award, unless the judges in that class placed some priority on originality.

American Concours candidates tend to be over-restored: detailed, painted, and chromed to a level far beyond that of the original. In Europe, originality is more valued, and unrestored automobiles, especially race cars, are often given high marks.

This was apparently the standard upon which the Eliminator was judged. My friend, Bob Wilson, better known as "Kermit" in vintage racing and car collecting circles, rushed up and announced, "Hey, they've called your name. The Eliminator has won an award."

"Jump in," I said, "ride over to the Judge's tent with me." Pamela at the time had retired to the Ritz's coffee shop, and Kermit was an obvious candidate as co-pilot for the short trip.

The Eliminator, set up for competition, had a clutch like a bear trap. Easy engagement was impossible as the big Chevy hooked up and angrily launched the relatively light— 1,900 pounds—old car.

Trying to keep the beast under rein, I slewed down the sodden fairways attempting to minimize the long divots produced by the eagerly spinning rear wheels.

The awards were being handed out by Hurley Haywood, the well-known Porsche race driver who had won Le Mans three times and was one of the finest endurance specialists in the history of the sport.

Our award would be a so-called "Amelia," a lovely eight-inch-high sculpture of an Egret—a majestic bird that populates the shores of North Florida. After receiving the trophy, I made a special effort to ease in the clutch to minimize damage to the turf.

I would discover later that I was less than successful.

When the Concours ended in the late afternoon, the fairways had to be cleared of automobiles. I mounted up once again and prepared to drive the Eliminator the short distance to public roads at the beach area compound where the trailers were stored. This caused me to become briefly mired into a line of cars departing the event. The holdup was a busy intersection leading out of the Hotel to nearby Fernandina Beach. Cars made the crossing one by one, and I found myself behind a new Mercedes-Benz sedan with Illinois plates. Because the Eliminator was not happy in traffic, I continuously blipped the throttle to keep its plugs clear and its coolant flowing. Starts and stops were fierce and jerky, no doubt causing concern to the Mercedes driver who must have thought the berserk vehicle in his rear view mirror was about to leap into his trunk.

This was a sufficient distraction for him to enter the intersection in front of a pickup truck, which bashed him in the right fender. This pile-up thankfully hurt no one, but managed to disable a perfectly fine Mercedes-Benz.

The responsible party was no doubt the Eliminator, whose bucking and snorting had rattled the Mercedes driver to a point where he had driven directly into the path of the oncoming truck.

Again the Eliminator could not be trusted in polite company.

But that was hardly the end of its depredations at Amelia

Island. The next morning I got a call in my room at the Ritz Carlton. It was Kermit.

"You hear about what you did at the awards ceremony?"

"What now?" I asked, fearing the worst.

"Remember how muddy it was?"

"Of course. That's why I tried to ease up on the clutch."

"It didn't work."

"Meaning what?"

"Meaning there was a lady standing behind the car in a white dress."

"Oh shit. Bad?"

"If bad is asking her to smile so they could find her face is bad, it's bad."

And so it went, disaster after disaster among the elites. The unruly old machine seemed to possess a personality its own, firmly linked to its past and its mongrel heritage. The junkyard dog had struck again.

We raced the Eliminator on an irregular basis with the SVRA for the next two years at places like Watkins Glen, Mid-Ohio, and Lime Rock. The drivers were two excellent choices: top-flight racer and Track Time chief instructor Tom Reece and veteran endurance driver and driving instructor Walt Bohren. Both drove the car with care and high skill, never putting a wheel wrong. Based on its history dating back to Duffy Livingstone's first drive, the car is believed to have spun only three times—all by Duffy—in its long racing career. During its resurrection, neither Skidmore, Reece, nor Bohren got so much as a wheel in the dirt—a testimony to their skill and the car's latent stability.

During its 50 years of life, only seven men had driven the Eliminator: Paul Parker, Duffy, Frank Monise (a Lotus-driving friend of Duffy's who had ran one Cal Club event), Bert Skidmore, Walt Bohren, Tom Reece, and me. Tom's vast experience in all types of sports cars and stock cars, and as chief instructor for Track Time—a top-rated driver's school—qualified him as an expert to evaluate the car, which he found to be amazingly stable. After a successful drive at a Mid-Ohio SVRA race where he finished third, Reece had the following observations: "This car was unlike anything else at the event, a definite edge with the spectators, as everyone likes to root for the underdog. The seating position is torso upright, legs bent at the knees straight down to the lowered floorpan (stay off the curbs if you like your feet). It's awkward to heel-and-toe. I quickly found the Eliminator was very happy with 'no clutch' downshifts. So the order was normal: upshifts with left foot braking and downshifts without the clutch exactly as I would prefer it to be.

"The steering lock is less than a half turn total, and you can imagine the effort involved in steering this around the track. It is never a problem while driving, but you know you have done something when you were finished. As for the drum brakes, they are friendly as long as you apply them slowly enough to allow all of them to 'energize' before hard braking. Otherwise you can find yourself abruptly changing lanes. The one thing that really stands out about the car is its handling. One would think that because of its primitive suspension it's diabolical to control. On the contrary: the corners seem to be where the Eliminator Special is most at home. You can drive it hard. Very hard. Be careful in the braking zone and go like *tihsepa* in the corners. An absolute blast!"

Because we faced newer, more advanced machines driven by the likes of Fergus (until he tragically passed away in 2000 due to the ravages of cancer) and John Harden, winning was never a possibility. But the old car continued to acquit itself well, finishing in the top five on most occasions. Once, we had to pull out, for there were tropical monsoons attacking Lime Rock that weekend, and we decided the risk was not worth the reward for yet another tin cup.

The Group Four competitors were a delightful bunch, often hosting little post-race parties at various competitors' trailers and generally enjoying camaraderie off the track. Vintage racing grows in popularity each year due to the ongoing fascination with older, noisier, rarer machinery and the ability to exercise them with relative safety. It was in this atmosphere that the Eliminator, Barry Brown, our drivers, and me were welcomed.

We made one diversion from road racing to the dirt ovals for which the car was originally destined by the late Jay Chamberlain. Thinking that it might be fun to explore the Eliminator's capability as a CRA track roadster, in August 1998 we entered the car in an Atlantic Coast Old Timer's (ACOT) event. The annual race was held at the St. Lawrence County Fair in the small city of Gouverneur in the Adirondack wilderness of upstate New York. Like most country fairgrounds, it featured an ancient half-mile dirt horse track with wooden fences and a quaint, white-washed timing stand. Historians believe that automobile races were last held on the old oval in 1932.

ACOT is one of many clubs devoted to the preservation of American oval track cars, primarily early midgets and sprint cars, with a smattering of early track roadsters, super-modifieds, and stockers. At this event, roll bars were permitted, but cages, which became universal in the early 1970s, were not.

The annual fair was underway when we arrived on that warm Sunday afternoon. The grassy infield had a group of perhaps 30 midgets and sprinters ready for a day of fun. ACOT does not allow outright racing, but rather lapping at controlled speeds, which can often stir the juices of the competitors. A number of such drivers, including the afore-mentioned Chuck Porter and Indianapolis veteran Cal Niday, have died while running these presumably low-key events.

By the time we had unloaded, there was trouble. In an early practice session, a few of the cars, throttling through turn one, tossed up rooster tails of dirt. Lining the fence on the outside of the corner were the midway concession stands offering up a standard carnival menu of hot dogs, burgers, cotton candy, sugared waffles, and snow-cones. The dust of the cars had enveloped the chefs and gourmands, causing fevered complaints to the authorities.

Because shifting was unnecessary on the oval, I was able to drive the Eliminator (gear changing for anyone with a shoe-size larger than a 10 produced the risk of getting the throttle foot lodged under the gearbox, which would disqualify the driver from road-racing.) As I belted myself in for a short heat race, we were summoned to a driver's meeting on the front straightaway. The St. Lawrence County

Sheriff ominously warned us that any more dirt tossing on the restaurants would mean instant expulsion of the entire ACOT group.

Properly chastened, we returned to our cars—a collection of aged sprinters, led by a neatly restored 1930s flat-tail sprint car powered by a GMC straight-six with three Weber carburetors. This was hardly an original set-up, but plenty potent for such modest levels of competition. We fired up, rolled onto the track for a pace lap, and received the green flag. The pace was supposed to be reasonable, with cautious passing.

But the St. Lawrence County Fairgrounds half-mile was vacant at the far end. Away from the midway and the grandstands, there was no fencing. Nothing except open field and scrubby woods were lining the fourth turn. As soon as we launched off the second turn, the race began. We hammered down the back straight and broadslid through turns three and four. Down the front straight we immediately eased off, theoretically to behave properly around the concessionaires.

We upped the pace on the second lap. They guy in the red GMC sprinter jumped out into an early lead. I lay in third, behind a 1960s-vintage, Chevy-powered sprinter. I drove through the third and fourth turns and into a cloud of dust. The leader had spun into the woods.

A red flag was displayed and we puttered into the pits. Meanwhile Barry, who was watching the proceedings on top of our trailer, spotted the red sprinter, which had arrowed through a small stand of trees and scrub brush to end up against a wire fence. From Brown's vantage point, it appeared that the fence wire was wound around the hapless

Sam Turner, partner in Eliminator Enterprises LLC. Brock Yates (center) and
Barry Brown(right), builder of the Eliminator.

Yates and Brown shake down the Eliminator. *Steve Rossini*

driver's neck. Barry leapt off the trailer, grabbed a pair of side-cutters, and rushed to the scene. He found the driver choking, the wire wedged against his windpipe. He quickly cut him free, perhaps moments before he choked to death. This once again proved that no matter where or when, all motorsports can be dangerous.

And in the case of the St. Lawrence County Fair ACOT program, it was also short lived. The Sheriff re-appeared, angrily announcing that we had again dusted the hot dog and frozen custard stands, and the event was officially cancelled. So much for the Eliminator's one and only appearance on a dirt oval. Duffy had once driven in a dirt hill climb at Tarzana, California—setting fast time—but never before or since has the Eliminator slid around a dirt track, despite Jay Chamberlain's early plans to compete at Gardena and Carrell Speedway. As luck would have it, the exposure lasted four laps or a total of two miles.

Exposure of another sort was accelerating. Numerous magazines, newspapers, and television shows were recognizing the Eliminator, including coverage by Speedvision and in the excellent British magazine, *Classic and Sports Car*. A major story appeared in the March 1998 issue of *Car and Driver* titled "Still Tihsepa after All These Years." Not only did it recounted the history of the car and its successful outing at Monterey, but technical editor Larry Webster also tested the old machine using the magazine's state-of-the-art telemetry equipment. The test was conducted on a chilly day at the Leicester, New York, drag strip with Webster at the wheel. The numbers were impressive for a car nearly a half-century old.

Zero to sixty came in 4.4 seconds while the quarter mile was run in 12.6 seconds at 115.6 miles per hour. Considering that the race-worn clutch was slipping slightly and the iron-hard Dunlop radials had a mere 6.5-inch-wide contact patch on a cold track that offered little bite, the times were impressive. Based on the data, final-drive ratio, and power-to-weight ratio, *Car and Driver* estimated the top speed at 150 miles per hour.

The old car returned to its favorable stomping grounds for the 2000 Monterey Historics. Again Bert Skidmore was assigned the driving chores. Before leaving the Riter Restoration shop, several modifications were made including the upgrading of the three Stromberg 97s to larger Rochester two-barrel carburetors and replacing Livingstone's hand-built exhaust headers with modern sprint-car style versions. This was done only in the name of preserving the irreplaceable originals in the case of a crash, not to improve performance.

We hauled the car west on an open trailer towed by my Stillen-modified Chevrolet dually pickup. Running with my son, Brock, Jr., and Barry Brown, we made the 2,800-mile trip non-stop and arrived at Laguna Seca in time for inspection and several practice runs.

This time the Eliminator was ready. We faced a strong field that once again included our old nemesis, the Silverman-Harden Lister Chevy, Rob Walton's (the heir to the Wal-Mart fortune and a fine vintage racer) superb Maserati Tipo 61 Birdcage, a pack of strong Ferraris and D-type Jaguars, Ernie Nagamatsu's famed Ol' Yeller II, and a fresh Canadian import, the early 1960s Dailu MK II of Mike

Leicester. The latter was Chevrolet-powered, with a light-weight tubular chassis, disc brakes all around, and what appeared to be fat Goodyear race tires, which was not permitted by the rules.

Despite being the oldest, crudest machine in the 10-lap race, Bert powered the Eliminator into fourth place in the early stages behind Leicester, Walton, and Harden and remained there for the duration of the event. He did however slow down during the final two laps, which led me to ask him after the race if the car was misbehaving,

"Naw," Bert answered, "I was going to lap Lou and I figured that wouldn't have made a whole lot of sense." He was referring to Lou Sellyei and his ex-Morgansen 250 TR Ferrari. Lou was a major customer of Skidmore's Intrepid Motorsport operation, and shaming a friend and a major source of business understandably was not prudent.

Slowly, the racing career of the Eliminator began to wind down. Both Brown and I had other projects and obligations that reduced the racing and car show appearances. Major discussion, were underway about yet another iteration of the Eliminator, and having already proven the point that the old car was still a potent competitor, it began to linger in a long-deserved rest.

Murray Smith, one of the most vivid presences in vintage car competition in the United States and Europe, had often expressed an interest in running the old car. We entered the 2002 Lime Rock Historics over the Labor Day weekend with Smith as the driver. Now promoted by Laguna Seca Historics impresario Steve Earle, the event was expected to attract a giant field of cars. Having been rained out at Lime Rock with Walt Bohren earlier, it was decided that a return might produce better results as well as exposing our new car (see Chapter 12).

Sadly, the Eliminator balked at Lime Rock once again. After two practice sessions, one by Smith and one by Skidmore to diagnose the weird handling, it was discovered that the right rear half-shaft keyway had fractured, leaving only the left wheel with power. This created intolerable instability, so the car was retired for the weekend.

At that point, the Eliminator was about to celebrate its 50th birthday as a full-tilt race car. It was time for retirement.

The car would continue to appear in exhibitions and at car shows of all kinds, but aside from an often-discussed trip to England for the Goodwood Revival and Historic races, its racing days were over. But in no way would this magnificent old war-horse disappear from the public view where it had brought so much pleasure—and produced so much bafflement over the years.

CHAPTER TWELVE
THE ELIMINATOR
SPECIAL AND BEYOND

Like every performance nut in the world, my involvement with the sport/hobby/profession/distraction/mania has ranged all over the automotive spectrum. Race cars, street rods, sports cars, motorcycles, snowmobiles, and fast boats have all been a part of my demented portfolio over the years, but I still had one unfulfilled ambition. I had never built an automobile that fitted my exact definition of broad-based uniqueness and performance, a vehicle that embodied both my interest in hot rods and sports cars, the kind of vehicle that Duffy Livingstone had so uniquely embodied with his Eliminator.

Once the old machine was back in western New York and Barry Brown, Sam Turner, and I had campaigned it at Watkins Glen and at the mildly disastrous St. Lawrence Country Fair fiasco, I began to think about other ways to expand its impact. Everywhere the car went, it seemed to elicit serious interest, and somehow that response demanded a greater effort on my part.

I began to scribble ideas for another car—a contemporary expression of the Eliminator—a kind of amalgam of old and new that expressed, in a sense, what Duffy might have built in the middle 1950s had modern drivetrains and technology been available.

There is a latent urge in all automotive nuts toward self-expression. It may be limited to simply a paint scheme or custom wheels or even, perhaps, vanity license plates. But the ultimate statement is a complete automobile—generally a hot rod, although a few people have enjoyed the resources or the will of a Carroll Shelby, Don Panoz, and Malcomb Bricklin and have actually embarked on limited manufacture of the car of their dreams.

The center of such self-expression lies in the hot rod and custom car world, where artisans, dreamers, eccentrics, and visionaries of all stripes have an opportunity to create rolling stock of their own. While many of these efforts are blatant copies of other people's creativity or else openly tasteless and ugly, some like street rod builders Boyd Coddington, Chip Foose, Roy Brizio, and others have elevated hot rod styling to a high art. Their work equals that of any issuing from the automobile industry's design studios.

My initial scribblings had one consistent theme; the elegant, almost angry nose created by Emil Diedt in 1951 when the Eliminator project was first started by Jay Chamberlain. This would be the key design element that would link the old car with the new.

I tried to develop a second generation car, or more correctly a third, in that Duffy had already built the Eliminator II, using an early 1929 T-bucket body. Several street rod firms offered 1924-replica fiberglass bodies like the original, but even with versions that offered a slightly lengthened cockpit for greater foot room, the accommodations were hopelessly cramped.

I commissioned Thom Taylor, the brilliant California automotive artist, to draw up some concept vehicles based on my ideas. While Taylor sketched a vivid shaped car, reservations about interior room forced a rejection.

I then drifted toward a classic Deuce roadster body, thinking that an all-steel Brookville replica might work. But more of Taylor's drawings left me with the impression that the car would end up a clone of too many other street rods. The 1932 highboy roadster had become such a standard element in the hobby that I sought, for variety's sake if nothing else, another venue.

Enter Barry Brown and Sam Turner, both of whom became deeply involved in the planning. Turner, who had recently sold his lucrative insurance business and planned to devote his spare time to vintage racing and other automotive diversions, became a partner in the new project. Eliminator Enterprises, LLC, was formed with the intent to build a prototype, expose it to the public, and perhaps build some customer cars on a limited basis.

It was an obvious decision that Brown's Riter Vintage Car Care and Motorsports would build the car. After long discussions with Brown and Turner, it was decided that a 1934

Ford roadster body would be used. It was perhaps the prettiest of the prewar Ford bodies, with a long sweeping trunk lid, and more importantly it offered plenty of interior room.

After consulting with Pete Chapouris about possible body builders, Wescott's Auto Restyling in Boring, Oregon, was the first choice. Their fiberglass bodies were steel-reinforced and known to be of high quality. As for the chassis, Total Cost Involved of Ontario, California, was a first choice, based on its reputation for quality and on-time delivery.

But what drivetrain? The standard-issue engine-transmission combination for contemporary street rods is a Chevrolet 350-cubic-inch V-8 hooked to a GMT 350 four-speed automatic transmission. This setup is ubiquitous, based on its cost, availability, reliability, and simplicity of installation. The 350 Chevy was a no-brainer, as it were, but we wanted something more unique and more importantly, we wanted an engine that would offer world-class performance.

This was based on our mission statement: build a street rod that was not simply a boulevard cruiser, but rather a truly high-performance machine with sports cars handling of the highest level.

I contacted Lou Patane, who was at the time handling the Mopar Performance Division of Chrysler Corporation. Arrangements were made to obtain a Viper V10 crate motor—a monster, all-aluminum V10 displacing 488 cubic inches and developing 450 horsepower and 490 pound-feet of torque. There was initial concern about the sheer size and bulk of the engine, until Mark Malmstead, a Chrysler engineer working within the Mopar Division, assured us that the

Viper, at 39 inches in overall length, was only a few inches longer than a standard Chevrolet small-block V-8 and, with its aluminum block and heads, about the same weight. Thanks to its fuel injection, the V10 was only 25.9 inches tall, meaning a lower hood could be designed than could be over a conventional carburetor setup.

The TCI contract was set, with wheelbase for the car planned at 118.5 inches to accommodate the rather long tail-shaft of the Viper 6-speed manual transmission. An automatic was out of the question, not only for performance considerations, but for reasons of size and weight. The only automatic offered by Chrysler was for its all-iron V10 pickup engine and was unacceptable—although several other hot rodders had attempted its installation.

Per our request, TCI fitted their chassis—powder-coated with a glistening black finish—with a Currie 9-inch Ford rear end (known to handle torque levels of the kind generated by a Viper V-10) and a rear coil-over suspension with Panhard Rod and gas-filled shocks. The front would be standard Ford Mustang II independent with similar shocks and rack-and-pinion steering. Brakes would be 11-inch Wilwood vented discs rolling on 15x8 front and 15x10 rear Lynn Park Trigo magnesium wheels and BFG Radial Comp TA 225 and 275 R/15 rubber.

When this setup was completed, the rolling chassis of the new Eliminator MK III Special was delivered to Las Vegas, where it became a featured element of the Mopar exhibit at the 1998 SEMA show. There it gained widespread attention and compliments for the excellent detailing by the TCI professionals. It was then transported 2,000 miles east to the Riter Restoration shops in East Rochester. There the real work commenced.

The Wescott 1934 roadster body had arrived, complete with five-inch channeling, the maximum available without total modifications to the inner structure. While Wescott hot rod bodies are considered to be among the very best in the business, it was found that ours was far from ready for instant installation if the results were expected to reach any level of acceptable professionalism.

Brown and his staff spent endless hours with the process called "blocking," a frustrating chore of aligning the body parts—the doors, trunk lid, seat mounting, and firewall—so that perfect symmetry could be achieved. This is an arduous and difficult job that simply cannot be avoided with fiberglass bodies, no matter how well fabricated by the factory.

In the meantime, a replica nose of the original Diedt masterpiece was sent off to Greg Rieggell in Gettysburg, Pennsylvania, to be reproduced in carbon-fiber. Gregg, a well-known East Coast fabricator of funny cars and other drag racing bodies, took on the job knowing that more bits were to come, including the hood and all four fenders, once Brown & Company, Turner, and I had agreed on the exact custom contours.

I wanted a look reminiscent of a late 1930s Bugatti or Jaguar SS100 sports car mated with a 1950s vintage hot rod. Extra Lucas driving lights and Brooklands windscreens, rarely seen on hot rods, were to be employed, perhaps with a

Nardi wood-rimmed steering wheel (although others argued for a Bell Indy-style four-spoked version).

Slowly the car took shape. A 20 gallon ATL fuel-cell mounted upright behind the cockpit and black leather upholstery graced the interior. The first attempt at paint was Viper blue while arguments continued over the color and trim. Jim Williams, who I had worked with at *Car and Driver* in the 1970s, contributed greatly to the conceptualizing. Taking time from his work at an advertising agency in Rochester, he also designed the first logo for the car based on my initial scribblings.

An attempt was made to adapt one of sculptor and hot rodder Stan Wandlass' beautiful 1932 Roadster windshields, but it would not fit properly on the 1934 cowl. We resorted to a Wescott cut-down, folding 1934 windshield that could be used in conjunction with Brooklands screens.

Slowly but surely the new car began to evolve into a real machine of the type I wanted, a true broad-spectrum performer and not simply a pretty street machine. With all due respect to the hobbyists in this field, many of their cars feature exquisite craftsmanship and riveting style but offer little in the way of real performance. Yes, a conventional 350 Chevy setup offers decent straight-line acceleration but not much in terms of cornering and braking power.

Years ago, when the Cobras were running at full cry, it was claimed that Ken Miles, Carroll Shelby's star driver, was able to accelerate and stop a 427 Cobra from zero to 100 miles per hour and back to zero in just over 14 seconds. That was a benchmark we sought with the "Eliminator Special," a throwback name to the 1950s Indianapolis era when all race cars were called "specials."

We immediately began to concentrate on the brakes. The Wilwoods supplied by TCI had to be fitted inside the 15-inch mag wheels. A call was made to Hal Baer, the Arizona manufacturer of excellent vented discs and powerful calipers essentially identical to those being offered on Z06 Corvettes and used on all manner of high-performance road and race cars. With larger Baer 14-inch diameter discs, larger wheels would have to be fitted. After a call was made to Halibrand Engineering, four replica magnesium bean-hole 18-inchers were on the way. The rubber would be Michelin Pilots.

Once the car was ready to roll, it was hauled west to the Cleveland suburb of Berea and the state-of-the-art shops of Corsa and Gil Marine Engineering. There, owner Jim Browning and his staff set to work installing their low-restriction mufflers and exhaust system of the type offered for Vipers and Corvettes. The Corsa exhaust is amazing in that it is relatively quiet at road speeds yet, under hard acceleration, offers minimum back-pressure and maximum performance. Catalytic converters were also installed to make the car road legal.

Both Eliminators, old and new, were then given a unique opportunity to stretch their legs on a sunny July 2002 weekend at Grand Island, New York,—a large lump of flatland splitting the Niagara River above the world-famous Falls. There, 50 years earlier, the Sports Car Club of America had organized a weekend of road races that attracted some of the top East Coast competitors of the day, including Ferrari drivers Bill Spear and Jim Kimberly. My father had taken me to the event where we hugged a wire fence on the outside of a right-hand corner. It is but a hazy memory, excepting the white-and-blue 4.5-liter 375 Ferrari of Spear, who won, and a few rumbling Cadillac Allards and fleets of buzzing MGs.

Now, half-a-century later, local enthusiasts revived the races as part of the Island's centennial celebration. A day of re-creation was planned on the old course, closed to public traffic. No pure racing would be permitted, owing to insurmountable crowd control problems around the 4.5-mile circuit. But lusty speeds on the various long straightaways were permitted, and we loaded up both Eliminators for a day of fun.

Barry Brown brought his girlfriend, Sherry (TK), while my co-pilot would be my son-on-law, Bob Lilly, who was visiting at the time with my daughter, Claire, and my two grandchildren, Sarah and Scott.

During the lapping session, both Barry and I found the new car to be amazingly docile at normal speeds. The clutch was smooth and easily to engage. The six-speed gearbox linkage was perfect. The big Viper engine ran cool in the 80 degree heat, and the brakes were solid and true. Despite what was obviously a bottomless pit of awesome performance potential, the Eliminator Special was a delight to drive in real world conditions.

The old car was another matter. It remained a wonderful, antediluvian handful. Its clutch was a bear trap. Its throttle linkage offered a simple, on-off choice of power and the steering, linked through its 70-year-old Dodge box, was uncertain at best. Yet hunched behind the machine's old Bell steering wheel, a few feet from its thundering exhaust, the original Eliminator was also a sheer hoot to run on the open road.

After the Grand Island outing, the Eliminator Special was ready for some real-world evaluation. This came at the Daimler-Chrysler Proving Grounds outside Chelsea, Michigan, on August 18, 2002, with *Car and Driver* technical editor Larry Webster at the wheel. The car was hooked to the magazine's advanced telemetry equipment that measured everything from acceleration to braking to g-loading in corners.

With former Chrysler performance engineer Charlie Henry on hand for consultation, Barry, Sam Turner, and I were openly tense about how the car would behave. While this was hardly a race, it was a moment when our claims, dreams, and fantasies about the car's performance would either be confirmed or "eliminated."

The test was inconclusive and not particularly rewarding. Zero-to-sixty came in 3.8 seconds, which was hardly slow, but less than we expected. Worse yet, the quarter-mile times were disappointing at 12.5 seconds at 114 miles per hour. Something was clearly wrong.

Seventy-to-zero braking was acceptable—without ABS— at 176 feet, but our skid pad numbers at 0.90g did not meet expectations. Excessive understeer was an added demerit.

We returned home puzzling about the disappointing numbers. The engine seemed down on power. The culprit was believed to be the installation of the air cleaners behind the radiator shell where they seemed to be out of the air stream. A call was made to old friend Bob Kennedy, an expert engine man whose shop, Kennedy Automotive in Niagara Falls, New York, featured a computer-controlled Dyno Jet-system dynamometer. He surely could trace what we believed to be a serious loss of power.

Chassis dynamometers have an advantage over conventional engine dynos in that power is read at the rear wheels, where the efficiency—or lack thereof—of the entire drivetrain (transmission, clutch, driveshaft, differential, brakedrag) is taken into account. The only X-factor that cannot be evaluated is aerodynamics and the overall coefficient of drag.

The Eliminator Special was mounted on Kennedy's pristine equipment, and his computer readouts were examined after each 30-second run. Our highest number was a feeble 336 horsepower. The trouble lay in the area of fuel or air starvation. With computer-controlled, fuel-injected engines, that is hard to trace. If there is a shortage of air, the engine-management system will automatically reduce fuel supply. Same for a lack of fuel, which will automatically reduce the air mixture.

Kennedy and Brown, like others who had examined the air intake setup, believed the power loss could be sourced there and not in the fuel supply. A quick alteration of the filters was made wherein the air supply was opened up. Voila, instant results!

We had found 92 lost horsepower. Power at the rear wheels jumped to 428 horsepower at 6000 rpm. Another trip to the test track was now necessary to determine exactly how well the car would really perform.

Autumn weather was closing in by the time we reappeared at the Chelsea Proving Grounds. Once again, Larry Webster hooked up his *Car and Driver* test equipment. The temperature hovered in the high 30s, with a raw wind blowing out of the northwest across the lower Michigan flatlands.

Seeking better skid pad numbers, we switched the Michelin Pilots in favor of stickier Toyo Proxes RA1: 275/35ZR18s at the rear and 225/40ZR18s at the front.

Despite the lousy weather, wherein the tires refused to reach operating temperatures and the skid pad resembled an ice rink, we were able to bump the skid pad number to 0.91g with moderate understeer. An acceptable number, but we wanted more when the weather improved.

The good news came under acceleration. The newfound horsepower knocked the 0–60 time to a lusty 3.5 seconds. Zero–100 came in 8.5 seconds and one 0–100–0 effort by Webster brought a time of 13.6 seconds. This was amazing, considering that ABS brakes are not part of the Eliminator package.

Sadly, the miserable crosswinds and plunging temperature inhibited quarter-mile times and aborted any attempts at top speed runs. Webster managed one pass at 11.9 seconds at 115 miles per hour. We believed the times to be inclusive. The car seemed capable of running in the low 11s with a top speed well north of 120 miles per hour. During the test, it took 13.4 seconds to reach that velocity.

No matter, the Eliminator Special generated times as quick or quicker than any current road car, including the most exotic Porsches, Ferraris, Vipers, and Corvettes. We want more, especially on the skid pad, as we seek to make the car the best handling, quickest street rod ever built. As this is written in the late winter of 2002, the goal is in sight.

EPILOGUE

The saga of the Eliminator is far from over. In faraway Grants Pass, Oregon, Duffy Livingstone continues to drive his Eliminator II on fine summer days in the Northwest. Back east in upstate New York, work continues on the latest iteration, the Eliminator MK III Special, to improve its skid pad performance, and we plan to return to the Chelsea Proving Grounds prior to stories in *Car and Driver* and *Street Rodder*.

More importantly, work will proceed on the old car to return it to its original condition, reinstalling the original roll bar, seat, valve covers, brake lines, oil pan, and other parts that had been updated for racing. This will be done in anticipation of an invitation to the 2003 Pebble Beach Concours d'Elegance, where it will be entered in a class for road racing hot rods.

This will be a rare and honored moment for the old machine. Its somewhat battered bodywork will remain unrestored. This may count against it when compared against more pristine examples in its class, but the mere presence of the car on the hallowed fairways of Pebble Beach is a sufficient capstone of the aged machine's lengthy career.

It will be retired from competition and future public appearances restricted to car shows and concours'. Meanwhile the new Eliminator Special will carry on, perhaps as more examples are built for enthusiasts around the world.

ABOUT THE AUTHOR

While best known for his columns in *Car and Driver* and his television reporting, Brock Yates has written numerous books, stories in major magazines, columns for websites and the *Wall Street Journal*, plus movie scripts for *Cannonball Run* and *Smokey and the Bandit II*. He is the creator of the famed Cannonball race and lives in the towns of Wyoming and Alexandria Bay, New York. He is the proud father of four children and two grandchildren. Vintage automobile racing consumes his rare spare time.

INDEX

The following is an excerpt from Brock Yate's Cannonball! (ISBN 0-7603-1090-4). It is available from MBI Publishing. To purchase a copy, call 1.800.826.6600, or else visit our website at motorbooks.com.

1971: The Madness Begins

peg the start of the entire cockamamie aVair at noon on a wintry day in New York, early 1971. I was on my way to lunch at Brew's Pub on 34th Street with *Car and Driver* editor Bob Brown and fellow senior editor Leon Mandel. Walking near the magazine's One Park Avenue oYces, it came to me, "Why the hell not run a race across the United States? A balls-out, shoot-the-moon, fuck-the-establishment rumble from New York to Los Angeles to prove what we had been harping about for years, for example, that good drivers in good automobiles could employ the American Interstate system the same way the Germans were using their Autobahns? Yes, make high-speed travel by car a reality! Truth and justice aYrmed by an overtly illegal act."

The early 1970s were a time when illegal acts were in style. Everybody was going nuts with causes, most of them against the law. The Vietnam War was at its crazed peak and everybody was protesting something. We were smoking dope. College guys were burning their draft cards and blowing up ROTC buildings. Blacks were marching in the South. Redneck Klanners were wrecking churches. They were rioting at Attica. George Wallace was yelling deWance at the Feds, as was Daniel Ellsberg, who gave the secret Pentagon Papers to the *New York Times* and was charged with espionage. Even the Army was in the act, destroying Vietnamese villages "in order to save them," massacring civilians at My Lai and drilling hapless students at Kent State. The entire system was unraveling. Peace and love was the cry in San Francisco's Haight-Ashbury and New York's Greenwich Village, where vile hatred of the "pigs," "the establishment," the government, and everybody over 30 was a life force.

Everybody was paranoid about everything. At *Car and Driver* we were convinced that the automobile as we knew and loved it was as dead as the passenger pigeon. Ralph Nader was at full cry, drumming his tocsin of automobile doom into the brains of the public, convincing them that that lump of chrome and iron in the driveway was as lethal as a dose of Strontium 90 or a blast from a Viet Cong AK-47. A few months before my idea for a race, Congress had passed a mass of legislation that was sure to transform our muscle cars and sporty machines into pallid, padded prams with all the visceral passions of a pint of yogurt. The Clean Air Act gave the automobile industry six years to cleanse its products of 90 percent of all toxic exhaust emissions. Worse yet, we were sure the new Environmental Protection Agency and the Occupational Safety and Health Agency—OSHA—were bound to unleash legions of nanny state bureaucrats on us with the sole mission of herding us into a mass of spineless, subservient humanity obedient to the will of Big Brother.

Such was the unhinged fear and loathing that pervaded the land in early 1971. Therefore, what better time to add to the national psychosis? We trekked along 34th Street with me preaching about the grand scheme of a race, to be named for Erwin G. "Cannon Ball" Baker, the greatest cross-country record-breaker of them all. It had been Cannon Ball who set all kinds of point-to-point records in the early half of the century, driving everything from motorcycles to lumpy, low-powered sedans, to supercharged sports cars, to dump trucks and army tanks, all run with his simple guarantee, "No record, no pay."

Baker, a craggy Hoosier with a big nose, a deWant smile, and a pugnacious jaw, broke into the business on motorcycles after gaining a ride with the Indian motorcycle factory team. He began to set open records, Wrst between small cities, then across the nation, which was still unconnected, coast-to-coast, by anything that could be described as decent highways. In 1915 he drove a Stutz Bearcat from Los Angeles to New York in 11 days and seven hours, an amazing time, considering that most of eastern California, Arizona, and New Mexico oVered little in the way of roads besides cattle trails and open range. On his way to setting 143 distance records before his death in 1960, Baker raced against the New York Central 20th Century Limited from New York to Chicago in 1928, beating the elite passenger train into the Windy City. His greatest drive came in 1933, when he drove *solo* across the nation in 53H hours, sleeping for a half-hour behind the wheel of his Graham-Paige Model 57 Blue Streak 8. Even today, with the two coasts linked by interstates, a one-man nonstop drive in that time frame would be a prodigious feat. But to do it on 1933-vintage two-lanes, many of them unpaved, borders on the miraculous. Therefore, what better man to celebrate in a madcap intercoastal adventure than Cannon Ball Baker?

Existential, high-speed drives across the nation were in style, at least in Hollywood. The most famous of them was the 1969 hit, *Easy Rider*, the drug-fogged chronicle of Peter Fonda, Dennis Hopper, and Jack Nicholson's motorcycle ride to doom at the Mardi Gras. In 1971 two low-budget pictures hit the screen, both of which became cult favorites, and one of which no doubt inXuenced my decision to run the Wrst Cannonball. Barry Newman starred in *Vanishing Point*, in which he attempted, for no apparent reason, to drive a Dodge Challenger from Denver to San Francisco in 15 hours. The second Wlm, *Two Lane Blacktop*, was trumpeted by *Esquire* (at the time at the height of its powers as an avant-garde literary journal) as "the movie of the year." It starred two rock stars, James Taylor and Beach Boys stalwart Dennis Wilson, as a pair of racers driving their beat-up, primer-painted 1955 Chevrolet hardtop around the country, making money from impromptu drag races. They hooked up with fabled character actor Warren Oates, driving a Xashy new Pontiac GTO, and dueled him in a mad dash on back roads to—in classic existential themes—nowhere for no real reason.

While *Vanishing Point* wasn't released until after the Wrst Cannonball had been run, the *Esquire* hype surrounding *Two Lane Blacktop* was a factor in my conception of the Cannonball.

Bob Brown was nervous about the idea. Mandel, always the dyspeptic contrarian, denounced it as childish and ridiculous. But Steve Smith loved it. Smith, my longtime friend and former fellow-staVer on *Car and Driver* during the glory years of the 1960s, and I had long been intrigued with the notion of long-distance open road drives as the ultimate test of automobiles. What better environment in which to evaluate cars? After holding the editorship of *Car and Driver,* Smith had drifted to Los Angeles, then back to New York and a copywriting job with the giant J. Walter Thompson advertising agency. When visiting Manhattan from my upstate New York home in the village of Castile, I always bunked with Smith, who, like the rest of us, was consumed with the fevers of antiestablishmentarianism.

We convinced ourselves that all manner of crazies, race drivers, hot car wackos, fellow journalists, etc., would immediately throw in their lot if a coast-to-coast Cannonball was announced. Aside from Baker's known records, legend had it that basketball superstar Wilt Chamberlain had driven a Lamborghini from New York to Los Angeles solo in 36 hours and 10 minutes. But Wilt had also claimed to have boVed women equaling the entire population of southern California, and there was no way of conWrming his time on the road or in the sack. John Christie, a former editor of *Car and Driver* who had defected to the Petersen Publishing empire in L.A., bragged about driving an Austin-Healey from Los Angeles to Washington, D.C., in 48 hours, which sounded impressive until it was acknowledged that he had counted only the time on the road and not his overnight stops. Any number of other so-called records Xoated around, but now it was time to lay down some legitimate times against a real clock. The concept would be exquisitely simple: Contestants would clock out of the Red Ball Parking Garage on 32nd Street (where the magazine housed its tiny test Xeet) in midtown Manhattan and drive, ad hoc, to the PortoWno Inn in Redondo Beach, (a noted racers' hangout) where they would clock in again. The lowest elapsed time point-to-point would determine the winner. This would be the Cannonball Baker Sea-to-Shining-Sea Memorial Trophy Dash. Here with an anomaly: While Baker called himself "Cannon Ball," I, for reasons I cannot recall, contracted the name to "Cannon Ball," thereby separating the late, great driver from the event, if only in name, but not in deed.

Who among serious car nuts could resist such a challenge? Everybody, it turned out.

Smith had read a story in *Rolling Stone* titled "Roaring Around with Robert Redford," in which the author recounted some high-speed driving by the actor. This prompted a letter from Smith to Redford. A surrogate responded indicating interest, then silence. Others in the car business expressed initial enthusiasm then began to fret about speeding tickets, punishment from employers, angry wives, etc., and steadily dropped out. We faced the prospect of a nonevent.

Our vehicle would be a 1971 Dodge Custom Sportsman van powered by a 360-cubic-inch, 225-horsepower V-8 that had been featured in *Car and Driver* as *Boss Wagon III*—the most recent of a series of vehicles that had been mildly customerized by the staV. *Boss Wagon III* became *Moon Trash II*, a paean to the well-liked, Manhattan-based Chrysler Corporation Dodge Division public relations expert, B.F. "Moon" Mullins. He was a good friend of the magazine and had arranged for the Dodge van to be loaned, after which it had been equipped with Scheel bucket seats, Cragar S/S mag wheels mounted with Firestone, 60-series Wide Oval tires, and other goodies, including a small Norcold refrigerator.

Two other drivers were recruited. I had met Jim Williams at a clothes-line art show in Rochester, New York, in the fall of 1970 and had purchased a painting of a sprint car he had done while Wnishing up his studies at the Rochester Institute of Technology. A Wne artist and Xedgling writer, Williams was on the verge of being hired by Bob Brown as an associate editor at *Car and Driver* and was an enthusiastic recruit for the Cannonball. A fourth, expert mechanic and club racer Chuck Kneugen, with whom I had campaigned in a Sadler Formula Junior and a Dodge Trans-Am car, was also set to run, but had to defer to a house-building project at the last hour. Kneugen's main contribution was to tune up *Moon Trash* and to install a small rooftop wing at my request—a disas-trous accoutrement that would not only slow us down but would butcher our fuel mileage in the name of high style.

With three drivers, there suddenly became room for my 14-year-old son, Brock Jr., who, while too young to drive the vehicle, would serve as an observer for cops—a sort of human adjunct to our secret weapon, a crude "Radar Sentry" radar detector that was at the time a state-of-the-art device against the rising employment of X-band radar by the highway patrols. The Radar Sentry was but one of a handful of radar detectors on the market at the time. All of them were essentially useless, although the police were limited to using stationary, hand-held radar guns. Antispeed technologies like Instant-on, K-and Ka-band, laser, etc., were unknown. VASCAR was beginning to be employed, but on a limited basis. The notion of using citizen band radio was unthought of and would not come into vogue until the middle of the decade.

Smith and I devised several high-speed cross-country strategies, including one ill-fated idea to run a straight-line Mercator-style route from upstate New York to Manhattan that dead-ended in a gravel pit somewhere in Bath, New York. After much planning, it was decided to take the classic route westward on the Pennsylvania Turnpike, across the Midwest to St. Louis, then angling southwest, utilizing as much as possible of the still-incomplete interstate system to Los Angeles. The symbolism appealed: The westward movement. To the Golden State! Hollywood! The streets paved with gold! Go west, young man! Look out, Horace Greeley, here comes *Moon Trash!*

Then came word from Redford. His secretary, a woman named Becky, called to say that he would like to go—Los Angeles to New York, if possible—but had a heavy Wlm schedule and wondered if the run could be postponed until August. A second call from a Redford surrogate named Ed Jones conWrmed that the actor was not available, although Kirk F. White, a Philadelphia exotic car dealer, told us he would provide a Ferrari Daytona for Redford, if he were prepared to participate. No dice. Redford was out. Other phone calls to friends in the business initially produced an agreement to race, but slowly each fell oV the wagon. Kim Chapin, the *Sports Illustrated* writer, dropped out after he lost a codriver. Jean Shepard, the New York-based humorist and fellow *C/D* columnist, demurred because of a heavy television schedule. Russ Goebel, the publisher of *Autoweek/Competition Press* claimed scheduling problems, as did Ford public relations man Monty Roberts, West Coast magazine writer Ocee Rich and hotshot advertising director/cinematographer Joe Pytka.

Worse yet, *Car and Driver* editor Bob Brown was getting nervous. He fretted over reader reaction to an overtly illegal race and began to waZe over coverage, although he Wnally agreed that I could write an extended column covering the event. As the proposed May 3, 1971, start edged closer, the race appeared to be devolving into nothing more than a solo run across the nation in an attempt to set a coast-to-coast record, if such a thing existed.

Once we decided to actually make the run, I wrote my monthly *Car and Driver* column for the July issue (two months early due to printing and distribution deadlines) just prior to leaving. It was there that the announcement was made for what would forever after be known as *Cannonball Baker Sea-to-Shining-Sea Memorial Trophy Dash.* A "trophy dash" was a short race, generally Wve laps, for the four fastest qualiWers in sprint car and midget competition and seemed an appropriately absurd play on words for a race several thousand times longer. "Memorial" was included in the title as a veiled lament to what we considered at the time to be the impending doom to high-performance cars and fast driving, at the hands of the government and the Nader forces.

In the summary paragraph of the column I made reference to some of the inspiration for the race: "Those fey sweethearts over at *Esquire* gave you the entire script of *Two Lane Blacktop* in a recent issue. Keep your eyes glued on this spot for the real thing. Maybe we'll call ours *Four Lane Cement*."

After installing several additional performance items to *Moon Trash II* in a shop near my upstate home, including a small racing-style wheel, Cibie driving lights, Fiamm air horn, a map-reading light and the above-mentioned rear wing, we made for Manhattan and a midnight start in front of Smith's apartment at 35 East and 35th Street. My log recorded the following inventory:

Steve Smith
first cannonball, 1971

Brock Yates didn't invent the Cannonball Baker Sea-to-Shining-Sea Memorial Trophy Dash. I did. Sort of. I've been a dedicated point-to-point racer since I was in boarding school, when I and the only other kid on campus who was allowed to have a car (he had a Porsche America 1300 Super coupe; I had a surplus World War II Navy Jeep) were given to making outrageous claims about how fast we could make it from the school, in Lenox, Massachusetts, to New York City. Nobody believed our speeds, so we dragooned two hapless under-classmen into riding shotgun as observers to certify the times. They returned blubbering about how we'd made them wet their pants, yada-yada. But to give you an indication of how "liberal" this school was, our antics inspired the headmaster (who drove a Wre-engine red '51 Chevy convertible) to try his hand at beating our record claims. We had to let him win: he was also the soccer coach.

Later, I organized (or, more fancifully, conjured) the Preppie Grand Prix, from P. J. Clarke's bar at 55th and 3rd in New York City to Dick Ridgeley's celebrated gin mill in Southampton, on Long Island, the twin poles of the protoyuppies' world, precisely 100 miles apart as the crow flies. Friday night, all the would-be Masters of the Universe would foregather at Clarke's (made famous as the watering hole in *Come Back, Little Sheba*), get well oiled, and then tackle traffic on the dreaded Long Island Expressway—a.k.a. "The World's Longest Parking Lot"—which did not then have a four-lane connection with the Sunrise Highway, the main thoroughfare of the Hamptons. The trick was to find the best shortcut between the LIE and the Sunrise. My theory then was to find the shortest stretch of two-lane, no matter how tortuous its path, that joined the main roads. It seemed to work . . . at least in my addled state.

In my early days at *Car and Driver*, I continued to expound the efficacy of the shortest distance between two points, and eventually inveigled Brock into attempting a new record between his house (then in upstate Castile, New York) and *Car and Driver* (then at One Park Avenue in the city) by laying a steel ruler between the two points on a topo map, tracing a straight line, and connecting a blue-veined network of obscure secondary roads that deviated the least from the theoretical mean. (Subsequently, this route proved to add no less than a couple of hours and probably 50 miles to the journey . . . duh!)

The genesis of a coast-to-coast contest was the number-crunchers' (Pat Bedard had replaced my choice, Pete Hutchinson, as tech editor of the magazine) insistence that the answer to the age-old question, "What's the Best Car in the World?" could be divined by reading the tea-leaves of acceleration, braking, and skid-pad figures. Yates and I, the Luddites, argued that a car geared for 110 miles per hour at the drag strip would be desperately noisy at normal cruising speeds; that tires capable of generating 1G cornering forces would dislodge your fillings traversing ordinary expansion strips; that racing-style brakes were treacherous unless you kept them up to operating temperature by dragging your foot on the brake pedal, etc. The Mercedes-Benzes of the era generated ho-hum numbers at the test track, we pointed out, but were clearly superior in over-the-road performance to, say, a Camaro Z-28. Moreover, I insisted, we could prove it.

The question was, over what road? And at what distance? I proposed that the techies race their choice (presumably a souped-up muscle car) against our choice (probably a Mercedes SL or a Porsche 911) from Brock's humble abode upstate to the infamous Red Ball Garage on 30th Street and publish the results. This idea faltered when it was pointed out that none of our readers would have the faintest idea of the road conditions between obscure Castile, New York, and the Big Apple. My next choice of a venue was New York to Florida, a route well publicized by *The Tonight Show's* bandleader, Skitch Henderson, who had regaled America with lurid takes of outrunning the cops (or, sometimes, not) in speed-trap-infested Georgia in his 300SL gullwing. The New York-to-Miami bogie was 24 hours or so.

Then I remembered that John Christie, a former editor of *Car and Driver*, had once claimed to have set a coast-to-coast record of 48 hours in an Austin-Healey 3000. Subsequently it was revealed that he had only counted the time he'd actually spent on the road, not the time occupied by the long-distance driver's essential "three esses" (sleeping, supping, and . . . well, you get the idea), and moreover, he had not driven from Los Angeles to New York, but had only got as far as Washington, D.C., before packing it in. No matter, the die had been cast. Coast-to-coast it would be, although I held out for Interstate 80, from New York to San Francisco, then the only cross-county route without a stoplight.

Once New York to L.A. had been chosen as a better benchmark (I had to concur: Southern California was the epicenter of car culture in the United States), I then, as the self-anointed navigator, fell yet again into the trap of the shortest-distance algorithm. Hence, the disastrous

Amboy "shortcut." Looking at a map, it was obvious that Interstate 40, the most direct route across the country from Oklahoma City westward, takes an unconscionable loop to the north after crossing the California border at Needles. Moreover, Yates had designated the PortoWno Inn *south* of L.A. as the western terminus (he had a friendship with Mary Davis, then the PortoWno's owner), and nobody wanted to brave L.A.'s murderous traYc on the infamous 405 Freeway.

Once again wielding my trusty straightedge, I reckoned that it would be best to start winding our way southward once we drew abeam of the famous meteorite crater at Amboy, and head across the high desert to connect with Interstate 10, which runs straight as an arrow into L.A. Only the peaceful hamlet of Twenty-nine Palms stood astride our path. Wrong! Twenty-nine Palms turned out to be a major Marine base, and we got mired in ADL (Anti-Destination League) traYc behind endless columns of six-bys, Mutts, DUKWs, M-113A1s, and Pattons on Xatbeds, thus ruining the spectacular average speeds we'd established up till then. At that point my mind went blank, and the journey became a bad acid trip.

About all I could remember from the previous 30 hours was setting the trip's fastest average speed during my Wrst stint (through Ohio, of all places), and realizing as we approached the California border that the powers that be took a dim view of bringing suspect produce into the Golden State. Having loaded the intrepid *Moon Trash* with baskets of apples and oranges (few of which were consumed on the way; we were too wired, and subsisted mainly on caVeine-laced chocolate bars), I desperately tried to jettison the excess as we approached the state line. I dimly remember motorists in our wake swerving to avoid the apples bouncing down the road behind us (I was squeezing them out the vent windows one at a time). And I remember Brock's wicked grin when the inspector leaned in and asked if we had any fruits or vegetables on board. "Only Smith," answered Yates.

That said, I have to admit Edison was wrong. Sometimes genius is 99 percent inspiration and only 1 percent perspiration. I did all the work inventing the Cannonball Baker Sea-to-Shining-Sea Memorial Trophy Dash, but *naming* it was pure Yates . . . and pure genius. I probably would have called it "The Cross-Country Race to Determine the Best Car in the World" and the event never would have been heard of again.

Longtime friend Steve Smith was a fellow editor during the glory days of Car and Driver in the 1960s before going on to high achievements in advertising and automotive journalism.

Jim Williams
1971

Here's to you, Mrs. Robinson. . . . On the eve of the Wrst Cannonball in the spring of 1971, I was 22, going on 23—mere weeks away from graduating from college. Today, when I encounter young men and women in similar circumstances, I'm amazed at how focused or at least practical they seem about their futures. I, on the other hand, was not unlike young Benjamin in *The Graduate*. I was unconstructively "concerned."

It wasn't a matter of not knowing what I liked. I liked cars. However, unlike the "like" that then as now is not uncommon among adolescent or postadolescent males, my interest was, in a word, pervasive. Years later, when asked by an employer (a large New York ad agency) to write something about myself as part of a pitch for a new car account, I started by saying, "Cars are the monocle through which I have always viewed the world. . . ." And unlike other occasional utterances in the ad business, this one was sincere.

I Wrst met Brock Yates in the fall of 1970. I had been exhibiting in an outdoor art show and sale that received coverage on the local Saturday evening news. The next day Brock decided to take his Ferrari Lusso for a ride and, having noted the event on the news, ended up at the art show, where he found me. He bought one of my sprint car paintings and invited me to visit him sometime at his house.

Beyond being honored and delighted to be invited, I had no expectations when I visited Brock for the Wrst time. He was an established authority. I regarded myself as a kid. Brock turned out not only to be a kind host, but actually indulged me with conversation on all manners of automotive stuV, including his opinion that Americans were losing their enthusiasm for cars. What was worse, we'd arrived at a point where cars had become safe and reliable. We'd built a highway system to allow for high-speed individual travel over great distances, yet we were less inclined to use and enjoy these fruits than those of the pioneer automotive era when cars were primitive conveyances and roads were virtually nonexistent. In fact, no one had really made a point of celebrating and seeing how fast the continent could be crossed since E.G. "Cannon Ball" Baker.

It made perfect sense to me. Besides, it was coming from a grownup with a house, a family, a barn full of cars, and a dog named Fred. It never occurred to me to question the necessity of a Cannonball Baker Sea-to-Shining-Sea Memorial Trophy Dash. And as Brock's plan for the event developed, I never seriously considered that I might be asked to participate. However, as the weeks passed, and as people began to wimp out, Brock eventually inquired if I would be willing to sign on as a reserve driver. "Absolutely!"

My family was a bit more circumspect. To allay their concerns, I paraphrased what I'd overheard Brock say to one or another nay-sayer on the phone, "If this was dangerous, or irresponsible, would Brock be taking his Wrst-born son?" It worked on just about everyone. But as I got out of the car at Brock's house on the morning the Wrst Cannonball was supposed to launch, I was reminded of young Ben, who ended up in bed with Mrs. Robinson merely because events had placed him there. Had I, too, been seduced by chance or inertia . . . or was this a bad dream come true?

The story of the Wrst Cannonball Run has been well chronicled elsewhere. For my part, I can say that I didn't do anything really stupid, and I don't think I said anything really dumb in the course of the actual run or on the return crossing. After all, Brock has continued to tolerate me as a friend for more than 30 years. Steve Smith still talks to me, as does Brock Junior, whenever our paths have crossed. Within a month of the Cannonball, I went to work at *Car and Driver*, not as an art guy, but as an editor. I would eventually serve as art director, but parted company with the magazine when it moved to Michigan. While with the magazine, I'd go with Brock on other driving expeditions—a banzai blast to Alaska in a Corvette, and a lap of America with him and another *Car and Driver* staVer, John Eberhart, in a 450SEL.

Was the Cannonball a good thing? I'm convinced the general auto-motive landscape of the last 30 years would have been a lot drearier without it. As for me, without it I, too, might have grown up to be a lot drearier. There was no sequel to the *Graduate*, so we don't know what might have happened to young Ben. But over the last 30-odd years, I've managed to eke out a living doing things with cars. And a couple of ex-wives notwithstanding, it's been a pretty good ride.

Thanks, Brock.

Jim Williams is a former staV member at Car and Driver *and a successful author and copywriter in the automotive Weld.*

Brock Yates Jr.
1971

The years removed most of the memories of this trip, though as a 14-year-old, wandering through the endless years of self-doubt and uneasiness that puberty and growing up provided, a few things are permanently etched in my mind. Lost are the recollections of the panic of looking for gas along the lonely, empty stretches of nighttime highways, the scrolling of an ever-changing America through the windshield, and the concern of my mother as we embarked. But I do remember it as a grand adventure, one I am profoundly proud to have participated in.

One of the more vivid memories was of an early radar detector, the Radar Sentry. Purchased by mail order from the back pages of some magazine, it was the Wrst one claiming to alert a motorist to the expense and inconvenience of a speeding ticket. I think everyone was optimistic about the budding technology. Clipped onto the visor, this little square box of strange electronics, instead of Wnding police lurking behind the overpasses, found every power line in the country. It was irritating and ineVective, and the consensus was to pull it from the windshield and discard it. Little did anyone guess at the time, it predates a whole industry of detection and countermeasures. I never leave my driveway without one now.

One of the biggest disappointments of the era of the Cannonball has to do with the 1979 running. Riding on the Wrst one, unable to drive, caused me to look for a ride for a future run. By the time of the last one, I had found a codriver with a Corvette willing to go. Of course, the timing was a secret, and having moved out of the house, I waited like everyone else for the announcement. This came as a surprise one afternoon while I was working. The phone call from my father was not what I hoped to hear. Knowing that I was six hours away from the city, he said the Cannonball was starting in two hours, and that he'd see me in a couple of weeks. I suppose this was my father's way of keeping me out of harm's way, but I do remember not being happy about it.

Perhaps I was too young, didn't have enough money to bail myself out of jail, or was otherwise just not ready for a banzai cross-country assault, but I do remember that conversation vividly. In the subsequent years, on each of my many trips across country, I think about the Cannonball experience, the eVect it had on my driving and the lessons we learned, at somewhat over the posted limit.

Brock Yates Jr. is the manager of the annual Cannonball One Lap of America and is a former class winner in that event and the Silver State Classic.